OPTIMAL
ENGLISH
GRAMMAR

Paul S. Lee

978-1461130017

Printed in the United States of America
First Edition

Recommendation

Designed for self-motivated learners of English as a second language, Paul S. Lee's *Optimal English Grammar* presents a review of the most fundamental aspects of English grammar in a concise and user-friendly way – without loss of detail or technical rigor.

*The book is organized in such a way as to reveal the author's acquaintance with language as an articulated system of structures and rules; this is a necessary perception in teaching any language – one that few books in the market highlight with so much clarity and explicitness. The reader can easily navigate through the book, organized by the major building blocks of a sentence. This book presents English grammar as something quite decomposable, able to be dissected and assembled, and so quite capable of being mastered.

The detailed explanations and examples in each chapter, coupled with error-identification problems and exams, will all guide the readers toward effective communication especially in formal settings (spoken and written), challenging them beyond the level of conversational fluency toward the precise yet creative and varied use of the language.

Optimal English Grammar is intended for self-study, but its benefits may increase if the learners are guided and assisted by competent English instructors. Anyone who wishes to optimize his/her English learning experience at his/her desk, THIS BOOK IS FOR YOU!

Jenny Lee
Linguistics Dept. Harvard University

Praises for *Optimal English Grammar* from Students

"For many years I had studied with various grammar books, but I still felt very uncomfortable in writing. Amazingly, after having studied with *Optimal English Grammar* by following the instructions and solving and analyzing extremely helpful questions in the book, I became very confident in writing, whether it is a professional article or a casual letter. To me, this book is like a compendious bible of English grammar. I believe that Optimal English Grammar is the only grammar book that will leave you fully satisfied. It is a must-read, a must-study, and a must-buy." – Sungsil Moon, Ph.D., a researcher at Center for Disease Control

"A non-native English scholar Paul Lee shares his knowhow with anyone who is interested - both natives and non-natives! *Optimal English Grammar* is the crux of more than 15 years of teaching and self-research. Although originally designed to help non-native students, Paul Lee's system will surely solidify and enhance native speakers' understanding in modern English grammar. The contents of this book are readily applicable to various fields of writing, including casual journals, short essays, and even scientific articles. The featured examples and questions are particularly helpful in highlighting the introduced grammatical concepts. Do I need to say more? This is the "OPTIMAL" English grammar book." – Joseph Kwon, MS II, Mercer University School of Medicine

"Even as a native speaker of English who had read and written extensively, I found *Optimal English Grammar* to be immensely conducive to my grammar skills. Covering virtually every grammatical concept in the English language, from the obvious and vulgar to the obscure and abstruse in a clear and succinct manner, the book challenged my grasp of the language, allowing me to fully master every important rule. The exams and examples especially helped with my preparations for the SAT: This book was a critical element for my receiving a perfect 800 in its writing sections. I fully recommend this book to anybody who wishes to expand his/her English skills." – Daniel Yoon, Chattahoochee High School

"In a few simple words, *Optimal English Grammar* is concise, comprehensive, and versatile enough to deal with any of the student's needs, whether it is the SAT, ACT, or simply a desire to get better at grammar. No matter if you've spoken English all your life or just started this year, this book strikes the right balance of substance and easy understanding for all to learn and gain thorough grammatical knowledge from."
– Casey Kim, Lambert High School

"Optimal English Grammar helped me a lot with the SAT, ACT, and TOEFL. This concise book has all the basic information the thick SAT and ACT books have and more!" – Junsoo Kang, LaGrange High

"Having lived in the States since I was 9 years old, I thought I had perfected English grammar by the time I first took the SATs. However, the scores proved that I needed a much more thorough review and practice. Following the guidelines provided by *Optimal English Grammar*, I was able to improve my scores dramatically on Critical Reading and Writing sections. I am grateful that I was able to study English grammar systematically and efficiently using this book before I lost the chance to see my true potentials." - Jiwon Kim, Illinois Mathematics and Science Academy (IMSA)

"I was fortunate to study with *Optimal English Grammar* that contains the most appropriate modern English grammar concepts and examples, both formal and casual, because language changes. The clear and laconic presentation of formal English grammar in this book helped me greatly, especially in the SAT preparation. I zealously praise this book!"- Aisha HyeRim Lee, LaGrange High

"As an immigrant from Korea who used *Optimal English Grammar* authored by Paul S. Lee, I strongly recommend this book to whoever needs to correct and reinforce his/her weak grammar skills and to learn essential details of English to prepare for any standardized tests. Clearly understanding both formal and informal English grammar from this book, I became confident in taking the writing and reading sections of the SAT." – Hyorin Lee, LaGrange High

"I think *Optimal English Grammar* is the most efficient grammar book in the world. To master English grammar, it is much better to go over this book a couple of times than to study with several other grammar books. This book is the quintessence of a grammar book. Simply the best!" – Soyun Kang, East Coweta High

"*Optimal English Grammar* is a book that, with its unique merits, distinguishes itself from other grammar books. It is the end product of the thorough process of getting rid of unimportant or unnecessary concepts and adding essential and beneficial concepts in unambiguous explanations. I thank this book because I became interested in mastering English grammar and was able to improve my English substantially." –Minzi Jung, LaGrange Academy

"Most books in the market are thick and wordy with complicated explanations: It is not convenient to study with those. However, *Optimal English Grammar* is extremely well-organized, and concise and easy to study with in addition to containing almost all the essential grammatical concepts. I praise this book!" – Juho Lee, LaGrange High

"I am convinced that this book will help improve English skills of countless learners by giving great examples and explanations so that the difficult English grammar can stay in the long-term memory. I absolutely recommend ***Optimal English Grammar***."
– Junseok Oh, LaGrange High

"It was just a few months ago when I was worried about my English-speaking life in the U.S. while my friends in Korea were already applying to colleges; however, that worry is disappearing now because of the amazing, visible improvement of my English skills by the help of ***Optimal English Grammar***." –Ashley Lee, Callaway High School

"I was one of the students who had struggled because of English. I tried in vain to search for a perfect book to get comfortable with English. But this book, ***Optimal English Grammar***, made English easy for me. Every page demonstrates the author's successful effort to let the reader understand the important grammatical concepts. This book made me a conqueror of English grammar. I wish many people receive the same kind of benefit from this invaluable book." – Julie Lee, LaGrange High

"English, which once seemed esoteric to me, has become understandable and usable since I started to study with ***Optimal English Grammar***. This book is awesome! I would recommend this book to all my friends. You will never regret if you study with this book. " – Seonhye Jang, LaGrange Academy

"***Optimal English Grammar*** is extremely well-organized. It has all the necessary examples that help understand grammar concepts. In addition to being invaluable in mastering English grammar and therefore in preparing for the SAT or the ACT, this book also helps the reader accumulate many nice words by starting with relatively easy words but using more difficult words as it progresses toward the end. I benefitted mightily from studying with this book. I loved this book!" – Josh Heebum Chun, Lafayette Christian School

"Concise, simple, and easy! ***Optimal English Grammar*** enables the learner to save a lot of time in mastering English grammar. Paul Lee is a genius, making this efficient book. I strongly recommend this grammar book." – Jaeho Lee, LaGrange High

Preface

For many years, I have taught English to numerous people from various backgrounds in both one-on-one and classroom settings. Even though I taught students from various national origins, most of the people I taught were either Korean immigrants, "the one-point-five" generation or the second-generation students, or international students who came to the U.S. to study English and other fields of study. These students ranged from elementary school students to college students, even though most of them were high school students who were preparing for the SAT, the ACT, or the TOEFL. One of the interesting facts that I learned from my teaching experience was that even the second-generation Korean Americans who were born in the U.S. consistently made many grammatical and word choice errors, especially in formal writing, because of the lack of a proper education and experience in English. Furthermore, my experience also taught me that the length of stay in the U.S. does not necessarily forecast one's level of English proficiency accurately. Some people who have stayed in the U.S. for more than 20 years still use elementary-school-level English whereas others who have stayed in the U.S.A. just for two or three years use as accurate and educated English as well-educated adult native speakers do. *— a past form of strive*

There are still many people both in the U.S. and in Korea who are struggling *to* with English and spending thousands of hours without satisfactory improvement on *put in* their practical and long-term English skills. As I strove to master and teach English as *efforts* efficiently as possible, I was able to accumulate a great wealth of knowledge about the optimal processes of mastering English. The word "OPTIMAL" is a very *most efficient* powerful word. It is derived from Economics and means "the most efficient," which, in the context of English study, can mean the smartest and the most effective way to master English as a whole in a given time.

The optimal English-learning method that I propose includes the following components:

1. Optimal Vocabulary Accumulation Method (using the Optimal Memoriza tion Method).
2. Optimal Pronunciation Mastery.
3. Optimal Grammar Mastery (through this book, ***Optimal English Grammar***).
4. Optimal Process of Combining All These Things in Everyday Life.

This particular book, ***Optimal English Grammar***, is devoted mainly to mastering The English grammar in the most efficient and easy-to-understand ways and includes concepts and explanations that I have accumulated throughout my English-learning, English-using, and English-teaching life in the U.S. Most other English grammar books on the market and English teachers have tried to seduce students with many preposterous illusions, one extreme case of which even offers a ridiculous method of "mastering English in a month"; however, they, in fact, give at most only short-term benefits that will disappear in a month. On the other hand, I can assure you that, if studied properly, this book will help you master English grammar in the shortest possible time and make it stay in your long-term memory, not just in your short-term memory.

This book will cover almost all of the important aspects of English grammar, ranging from very basic grammatical concepts and rules to various, hard-to-understand exceptions and challenging concepts in the most concise presentation. To do that, I took out some of the relatively insignificant details and redundant examples that most other Grammar books hold onto, and added instead more important and practical concepts, examples, and explanations. Furthermore, for conciseness and effectiveness, I efficiently categorized grammatically important concepts and words so that the learners can not only optimally absorb them but also find the place to look at and refer to. In this book, I tried to teach the kind and level of formal grammatical knowledge that is necessary and sufficient for success on standardized tests such as the SAT, ACT, TOEFL, GRE or LSAT, which I believe is sufficiently effective and rigorous as well as practical, even though I commented on casual usages as well. For people who have only a small amount of vocabulary, I also tried to use relatively easy words in my examples and explanations in the beginning and then use more difficult words toward the end.

I believe that after completing this book and optimally reviewing it, by following the OMM method which is explained in the Appendix, you will see English with a very different and more accurate eye and use English with supreme confidence.

Paul S. Lee   (이상현)   **March, 2011**

Acknowledgements

I would like to thank my students who have helped make this book better by their honest and creative comments and questions. I also wish to thank Jenny Lee, my friend and a great linguist from Harvard, for sharing her expertise and providing helpful suggestions, and Ju Hyun Lee, my friend and a competent book designer, for trying to make this book visually optimal as well.
I also thank my family, including my spiritual family, who fully supported this project with their encouragements.

All remaining errors in this book, if there are any, are my own.

OPTIMAL ENGLISH GRAMMAR CONTENTS

OPTIMAL ENGLISH GRAMMAR
PART 2 *STYLE*

Appendix 1

You may skip this Appendix and begin studying Optimal English Grammar that begins from Chapter 1. But the OMM method explained in this Appendix might prove very useful in optimally transferring the grammar knowledge that you will learn in this book to your long-term memory. Read at least the last paragraph of this Appendix to study Optimal English Grammar in the optimal way!

An Essential Pre-Grammar Advice: "Building a Solid Long-Term Vocabulary Stock in Your Brain is the Most Important Task to Master a Language."

There are two essential components in any language that you want to master: vocabulary and grammar. Vocabulary can be described as the stock of words and idioms (an idiom is an expression whose meaning cannot be understood by combining the meanings of its constituent words). Grammar is the set of rules by which words are linked together to achieve efficient communication. We can think of vocabulary as pearls and grammar as the gold chain that connects the individual pearls to create a beautiful, and much more valuable, necklace.

Whether it is Reading, Writing, Listening, or Speaking, vocabulary and grammar are the essential and sufficient ingredients to perform these activities. However, some students of mine have said that they are good at both vocabulary and grammar and yet cannot speak or write well. However, such a reflection stems from their limited understanding of the nature of "vocabulary" and "grammar." If you have truly mastered vocabulary and grammar, you couldn't feel uncomfortable with some of these activities. When we talk about "vocabulary," we ought to include all of the components that constitute vocabulary: spelling, pronunciation which includes accents, and precise definitions and usages along with, for the application of proper grammar, its parts of speech. Therefore, when people say that they do not feel confident in English, it simply means they haven't really mastered vocabulary or grammar. This used to be the most frequently observed problem for Korean students, especially those who receive very high scores on tests like TOEFL but still perform poorly especially in some or all of the areas of speaking, writing, and listening (this is starting to disappear, however, since the current TOEFL iBT style tests all four activities of English Language: reading, writing, listening, and speaking). The problem is still their vocabulary and grammar because, to be able to use a language effectively, there is nothing else to study but vocabulary and grammar. The problem is that they didn't make their vocabulary and grammar usable enough or because they didn't put them in their long-term memory and thus forgot them fast. Again, as a final emphasis, vocabulary and grammar are the necessary and sufficient conditions for mastering English as a whole.

On the other hand, even though both of these components are essential, the vocabulary acquisition process takes a whole lot more time (in my opinion, about 50 to 100 times more) than grammar mastery process because there is no limit to the size of vocabulary. Even when you want to memorize, for the purpose of practical use, 10,000 to 20,000 words and 1,000 to 3,000 idioms (beyond which it is not really of great practical importance since you rarely use them in everyday life; moreover, this vocabulary level is enough to ensure that you will have no problem in reading and understanding most books, except some professional books), the time a person with an average intelligence invests to store them in his/her long-term memory is at least two thousand hours whereas for grammar it can take less than 100 hours. Furthermore, with the help of *Optimal English Grammar*, a person can master English Grammar in much fewer hours. In addition to great grammar books, you can benefit tremendously from outstanding teachers in learning grammar. However, the teachers' contribution in transferring vocabulary into your brain is not as great even though the teachers can clarify some vague definitions, correct wrong pronunciations, or motivate you to try harder to memorize and acquire more vocabulary, etc. Bearing in mind that this extremely important task of vocabulary accumulation takes considerable time and effort, let's find out the optimal vocabulary accumulation process.

Optimal Vocabulary Accumulation Methods (OVAM)

There are many channels through which you can accumulate vocabulary. The following diagram shows some of the possible effective ways of increasing your vocabulary stock.

Of course, the best way would be to use all these channels optimally. Depending on the learner's age and disposition, the main concentration of your effort can change, but still you will get the greatest result if you can somehow manage to do all these activities.

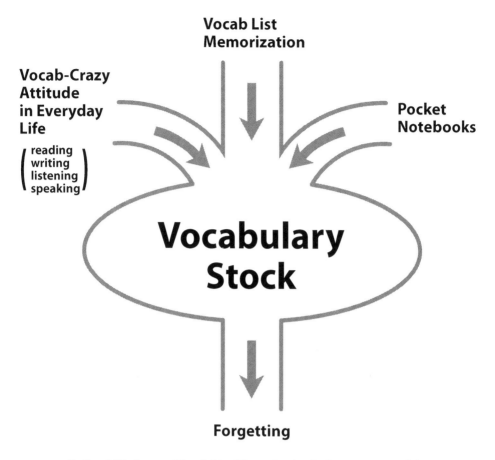

Vocab List Memorization

Vocab-Crazy Attitude in Everyday Life

(reading writing listening speaking)

Pocket Notebooks

Vocabulary Stock

Forgetting

- *Optimal Dictionary/Vocab List Memorization* is the most powerful vocabulary accumulation channel for the people who are very good in Korean/other language and want to gain the most English words in the shortest amount of time. In my teaching experience, those who had persevered in this challenging and time-consuming process significantly improved their long-term vocabulary. In this method, you memorize the easy and essential vocabulary first. For example, most of the English-Korean dictionaries nowadays use the following signs to indicate the frequency levels of their entries:

    1. The cross sign (+) or three-star sign (***,usually vertically stacked up) -- these words are the most fundamental words used every day. Usually, there are about 1500 to 2000 words in this level, depending on the dictionary you use.
    2. Two-star sign -- these words are very frequently used in America. If you can utilize these words perfectly, you will not have much problem

while staying or living in the U.S. Usually, there are about 4000 to 4500 words.

3. One-star sign -- these words are still used often but not as frequently as the first two levels. This is approximately the level of vocabulary of an average American 12th grade high school student. Most educated Americans know almost all of these words.

Personally, I recommend using small dictionaries for concise definitions and portability. Studying with a small or medium size dictionary is recommended when you want to start by memorizing these fundamental words. I would say that these 12000 words are essential words you have to master as soon as possible to make yourself comfortable with reading, writing, listening, and speaking in English. This vocabulary level used to be enough for TOEFL (the Test of English as a Foreign Language). For higher-level vocabulary, you can use other great vocabulary lists or books using the optimal memorization method that I am about to discuss. If you want to take the SAT, GRE, or LSAT, you definitely have to learn beyond this level. I personally recommend Barron's SAT or GRE Master Word List that consists of about 3,500 SAT-worthy words. And for the one-point-five generation or the second-generation students in the U.S.A., I recommend, for starters, Paul S. Lee's Customized Vocabulary Lists (level-1 vocabulary list and level-2 vocabulary list) along with Newbury House's or Longman's or Oxford's American English Dictionaries for their concise definitions and example sentences.

Anyway, if you consistently concentrate on this task 2 hours a day for one year, it is possible to put as many as 10000 words in your long-term memory. You can accomplish this even faster if you use these words in your everyday life. This level of vocabulary is, in my opinion, what an average native-born American adult has in his/her brain. However, you should be a bit more ambitious if you want to be internationally successful in your career.

- ***Using Pocket Notebooks*** is also a very powerful channel. Those who are under the age of say 10 might learn vocabulary more effectively by concentrating on this channel than on the dictionary memorization. A pocket notebook is a hand-sized notebook that has about 50 to 100 sheets. You basically write down any decent words that you encounter in your life from reading books, listening to your teachers and friends, or watching TV. Then you write down their definitions when you have access (preferably all the time) to a dictionary and study with it whenever you have time, even very short periods of time. There are two aspects that make studying with pocket notebooks very efficient:

1. The words that you enter into your pocket notebooks are those that you encountered in context. So it is much easier to memorize these words than to memorize from a list of words that you have never seen or heard before. With adequate review of the words in your pocket notebooks, you can transfer these words to your long-term memory with a small number of repetitions.
2. You can utilize every little bit of time in studying the pocket notebooks. Since a pocket notebook fits in your pocket, you can study it while walking on the street, eating alone, waiting for or riding on a bus, and so forth. You can study it easily even when you have only a couple of minutes. So every little piece of time can be transformed into a very productive time for building up your vocabulary stock.

Completing 20 pocket notebooks will almost transform you into a walking dictionary. Use the following OMM to transfer these words into your long-term memory. You may take advantage of portable modern devices such as smart phones or smart pads to compile your own pocket notebook lists.

- *Vocabulary-searching attitude in everyday life* is probably the most important aspect of OVAM, especially for those who are studying English in an English-speaking country. The reason is that you can basically utilize all of your time (or to be more precise, your non-sleeping hours) for vocabulary accumulation. If you read a lot, you will gain a lot of words automatically. If you keep track of these words optimally, your vocabulary will grow even faster. There are people who reached a sufficient level of vocabulary simply by reading quality books without having to memorize any vocabulary list. This attitude, coupled with the pocket-notebook method, will allow you to remember better all the words written in the pocket notebooks, and, of course, you will write more words on the pocket notebooks if you have this attitude. Furthermore, with this attitude, dictionary memorization process will become much faster and easier, too.

So using and combining all these methods will keep inflating your vocabulary stock at the maximal pace by a powerful synergy effect.

Optimal Memorization Method (OMM)

This method is the most powerful and efficient method to make your long-term or permanent knowledge base grow.

I have created and developed this OMM based on my English-learning and English-teaching experiences as well as the knowledge I gained from a Human Memory Class at the Johns Hopkins University. This method is the most powerful and efficient way to increase your long-term or permanent knowledge base. You can apply this method to any kind of study in which you have to memorize lists of definitions or concepts. The following three concepts or processes summarize this method.

1. ***The Sectionalization Process:*** This process is very important because an average or even a very smart person has a limited memory-span. In other words, it is better to divide the whole list of words into sections, subsections, subsubsections and so on. This ensures that you memorize the words solidly enough without later saying, "I don't remember these at all" when you review them. This process is closely related to the following ***Checking/Marking/Screening Process.***

2. ***The Checking/Marking/Screening Process:*** These three words describe fundamentally the same thing. You want to "ELIMINATE" the words or concepts that you already have in your "LONG-TERM" memory. Long-term memory can be understood as the memory or database in your brain that will not be wiped out or forgotten for many years. For example, if you think that you won't forget the word "house," then you can assume that it is stocked in your long-term memory. For efficiency, you should not review this word in the future because it will most likely be a waste of time. However, for the words that are in the short-term memory, you have to review and repeat them properly to move them quickly to your long-term memory. By this process, you can screen the words in the long-term memory from those in the short-term memory and focus only on those weak words that are in the short-term memory. How to carry out this process will be explained nicely through an example and illustrated by the following diagram. A very important thing to remember is that you have to give at least one or two weeks of no-review period before you do the next checking process because only after a sufficient time interval are you able to distinguish accurately enough the words in the long-term memory from the words in the short-term memory.

3. ***The Repetition/Review in Increasing Time Intervals:*** The mechanism behind this method is beyond the scope of this page, but it has proven really effective from my own experience and from the experiences of the students I have taught. You basically want to wait optimally before you review and solidify the

memory to maximize the efficiency of memorization. Giving too long an interval *just a period of time* can result in the loss of memory; giving too short an interval is not the most ef- ficient because of the suboptimal repetitions. Therefore, you have to apply optimal *true.* intervals between reviews, usually increasing intervals, as the memory becomes *between two events* more solidified.

to make solid and hard *lower than optimal*

Applying the OMM: An Example Using Dictionary Memorization Process.

You may skip this section unless you want to apply this method right now to your vocabulary accumulation process.

Suppose you are trying to memorize the two-star words in a good dictionary. There are about 4500 such words and suppose you know about half of them (an average Korean high school student in Seoul would know about this much from my experience). So, for now, suppose that you have to memorize a 2000-word list from this dictionary.

1. Then the first thing you have to do is the Sectionalization process. You want to divide the 2000 words into, say, 4 sections, each of which contains about 500 words. Then for each section, you want to divide it into, say, 5 subsections, each of which contains about 100 words. Then you divide each subsection into 2 subsubsections, each of which contains about 50 words. Finally you divide each subsubsections into 5 subsubsubsections each of which contains approximately 10 words. So you have sectionalized the list of 2000 words into very small subsubsubsections of 10 words. You don't have to count the words. In more practical terms, suppose that you are memorizing words from a dictionary which is about 1000 pages. Then you will have about 2 words per page that you don't know. Thus about 5 pages can be considered a subsubsubsection and 25 pages can be considered a subsubsection.and 50 pages, a subsection. Because most letters of the alphabet, other than C and S, which contain about twice as many words as most of the other letters, are about 50 pages long, give or take 10 pages, a letter can be considered a subsection for you. And A through C, D through K, L through R, and S through Z can each be considered a section.

2. After this brief sectionalization, you want to start memorizing. But before you actually get into memorizing, you want to eliminate the words that you know for sure by applying the Checking/Marking/Screening Process. This, I call the "FIRST CHECK". Using a blue pen, for example (whichever is easier to distinguish), draw a little dot right before the word that IS NOT IN YOUR LONG-TERM MEMORY and do this for one letter, which is a subsec- tion. Then try to memorize the marked words only.

3. Okay, now you have marked one subsection that contains about 2 subsubsections and about 10 subsubsubsections. You want to memorize the first subsubsubsection of about 10 words first. Spend about 5 to 20 minutes, depending on your intelligence, in memorizing from word #1 to the last word in this subsubsubsection and then spend 3 to 5 minutes in

reviewing them. ONE THING YOU HAVE TO MAKE SURE IS THAT YOU MEMORIZE EACH WORD WITH **ITS PRONUNCIATION** ALONG WITH A **CLEAR UNDERSTANDING OF THE WORD'S DEFINITIONS** (USUALLY THOSE DEFINITIONS WRITTEN IN BOLD FACE ARE ENOUGH OR THE FIRST COUPLE MEANINGS) AND **ITS PART OR PARTS OF SPEECH.** Then repeat this process with the next subsubsubsection and then **COME BACK** to the FIRST subsubsubsection and review it for 2 to 3 minutes and then review the SECOND subsubsbusection for 2 to 3 minutes. Then go to the THIRD subsubsubsection and do the same process and **COME BACK** to the SECOND subsubsubsection to review and so on until you finish the first five subsubsubsection to finish up the first subsubsection, which is about one half of the entries belonging to the letter A or B. Now the time to complete this subsubsection is in total from 50 minutes to two and a half hours depending on your intelligence at the moment (intelligence changes over time; the more you use your brain, the more intelligent you become). So spending approximately one to three hours a day can transfer about 50 words into your semi-long-term memory. They might not be in your long-term memory yet unless you review them later properly in the following manner.

4. The basic daily amount is this subsubsection. Then do the SECOND subsubsection the next day in the same manner and review the FIRST subsubsection by browsing through it for about 20 minutes and on the next day review the SECOND subsubsection. The process described until now completes one letter of the alphabet, which is a subsection.

5. Now repeat this process (from 2-4) for the SECOND letter, i.e., the next subsection. Then review the FIRST letter again. Then go to the THIRD letter and memorize the words using the same process as the previous letters.

6. If you go on like this, spending one to three hours a day, you will be able to complete one section, say A to C, in one week. Pretty fast, right? But you can't consider all of them to be in your LONG-TERM memory yet. So by the time you start the next section or D to K, you want to start doing the "SECOND CHECK" on the "FIRST-CHECKED" words in A. The key to this checking process is that you give yourself enough time (i.e. enough no-review time) to screen out the words that were transferred into your long-term memory from the words that weren't. So if you have forgotten or are not absolutely sure about some of the words that you studied, you "SECOND-CHECK" those words by underlining them with, for example, a red pen. Then memorize only those second-checked words. If you followed my prescription and took effort, then you normally would second-check fewer than 50% of the first-checked words. In other words, you are able to eliminate 50% of the first-checked words. They are not your concern now because they are safe in your long-term memory even though a very small percentage of them might be on the borderline, but this problem will be taken care of when you do the final check.

7. Now that you second-checked A and memorized them again, you start the first-check process on D and do the second-check process on B and do the first-check process on E and do the second-check on C and finish up the rest of the D-K with the first check process.

8. When you are starting the third section, which is L-R, start doing the second-check process on the second section like how you did before with the first section. And do exactly likewise

with the last section which is from S to Z.

9. When you finish first-checking Z, start the THIRD-CHECK process from A by, for example, circling around the word. Again you third-check only among the second-checked words (i.e. red-underlined words) and memorize those.

10. Now when you finish the third check, you would probably have eliminated 90% of the initial first-checked words. So among the 2000 words that you didn't know for sure, you got them down to about 200 third-checked words most of which will be memorized completely by the third-check process.

11. Now after the third check, give about a month or two before you do the final FOURTH CHECK. This final fourth check is a bit different from the other checking processes in that you can fourth-check not only out of the third-checked words but also out of all the first-checked words. In this way, the words that were at the borderline and not third-checked can be fourth-checked and get another chance to be memorized into your long-term memory.

12. So following this OMM, an average person will be able to memorize perfectly all 2000 words or all the two-starred words in fewer than two months simply by investing just one hour every day. And if you are a bit slow, you can still finish it in two months by spending two or three hours a day. And the vocabulary you built through this OMM will be so powerful that you won't forget it for many years and you will be able to use it appropriately with correct pronunciation and usage. 99% of them will be in your LONG-TERM memory for you to use anytime. Congratulations!!!

You can apply this process to any list of words you have to memorize by adjusting a little bit depending on the length of the list or its difficulty level. You basically do the same thing on the more challenging one-starred words after you complete the two-starred words. In fact, you even can use this method on any kind of study in which you have to memorize or understand a list of concepts, be it any language, mathematics, science, or even Bible verses. This is indeed, for most people, the most powerful and smartest method of increasing the LONG-TERM knowledge base of essential information.

The following diagram summarizes all the steps from 1-11. Here, the letters A, B, and C in the diagram represent different actions, not the letters of the alphabet. Action B consists of 5 Action A's and the interim review processes. For example, action A is like memorizing a subsubsubsection of 10 words; action B is like memorizing a subsub-section of 50 words; and action C is like memorizing a subsection of 200 words. The small slashes represent the review effort of each word. The horizontal axis represents the time progression.

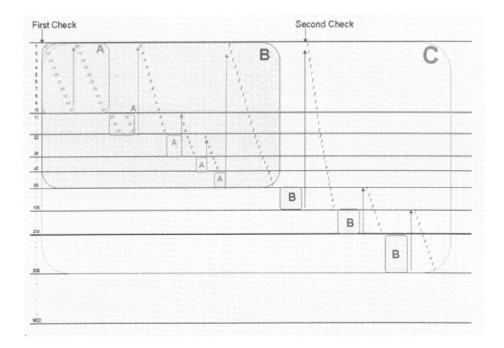

Read the following before beginning *Optimal English Grammar.*

After understanding this method completely, apply this OMM, with a little bit of flexibility and adjustment, to this **Optimal English Grammar.** First, underline or mark the parts in which you are not 100% sure of the concepts or explanations mentioned therein, paying special attention to <u>Notes</u> and Errors/Corrections (they contain important and challenging concepts that appear often on the SAT/ACT). That is going to be your first checking/marking/screening. The sections are divided nicely in numerical numbering systems with sections, subsections, subsubsections, etc. After completing and studying this book, give about 3 weeks as a no-review period. Then after that period, second-check with a different color among the parts that were first-checked and so forth until you third-check the entire book and study those parts. And by that time, you will have absorbed all the contents of this book into your long-term memory and wield that powerful knowledge as you want. Pre-Congratulations!

OPTIMAL ENGLISH GRAMMAR

Part 1

PARTS OF SPEECH

1   Basic Concepts

What is grammar? As mentioned before, grammar is like a gold chain that connects pearls to make an expensive and valuable necklace: Grammar connects words to make powerful and efficient sentences. It is generally considered as a system of rules that applies to a language. However, in a practical sense, when people say that they are studying grammar, they are investing the majority of their time on studying the exceptions to general rules rather than the rules themselves. So the majority of this grammar book will in fact be devoted to studying these exceptions because the general rules themselves are neither many nor difficult. In this short chapter, let's study and review the most fundamental general rules and concepts of English.

A Simple Review

There can be as many patterns in English Grammar as you want to name, but all the sentences in English can be categorized into one of the following five basic patterns. The part of speech that distinguishes these patterns is the VERB in the predicate; every sentence falls into one of these basic patterns based on the nature of the main verb (the verb of the independent clause) it uses. Now, before you get into these patterns, you want to be clear about the concept of clause. A clause is a chunk of words that contains both a subject (even though sometimes it may be omitted) and a verb. We have two kinds of clauses: independent clause and dependent (or subordinate) clause.

- **Independent clause:** a clause that can stand by itself and can form a complete sentence by itself.

- **Dependent (Subordinate) clause:** a clause that cannot stand by itself and needs an independent clause somehow attached to it to form a complete sentence. This clause starts with a subordinating conjunction such as *when, before, while, since, if, that, which,* etc.

Now with these two kinds of clauses, you can form four sentence types:

- **Simple Sentence:** a sentence that contains only one independent clause.

  Ex) I am going to school.

- **Complex Sentence:** a sentence that contains one independent clause with one or more dependent clauses.

  Ex) I am going to school after I eat my breakfast.

- **Compound Sentence:** a sentence that contains two or more independent clauses connected by coordinating conjunctions such as *but, or, yet, for, and, nor, so* (**BOYFANS** as a mnemonic acronym).

  Ex) I am going to school, and my friend will be waiting for me

- **Compound Complex Sentence:** a sentence that contains two or more independent clauses and one or more dependent clauses.

  Ex) I am going to school after I eat my breakfast, and my friend will be waiting for me.

Let's use simple sentences to analyze the five basic patterns.

1.1 Five Basic Sentence Patterns

1.1.1 Basic Pattern 1 (BP1) – Complete Intransitive Verbs

> **STRUCTURE: [SUBJECT] + [VERB]**
> **EX) [THE BIRD] [SINGS].**

Complete intransitive verbs are verbs that can stand alone or that do not use an object or a complement.

Ex) sing, walk, sleep, stand, frown, snore, smile, etc

The part of speech that can come in the subject's place is noun or pronoun.

1.1.2 Basic Pattern 2 (BP2) – Incomplete Intransitive or Linking Verbs

> **STRUCTURE: [SUBJECT] + [VERB]**
> **+ [SUBJECTIVE COMPLEMENT]**
> **EX) [THE WORLD][IS][VERY BEAUTIFUL]**

Incomplete intransitive verbs are verbs that use a subjective complement but not an object.

Ex) be-verbs, grow, turn, become, get, look, sound, smell, taste, feel, etc.

The parts of speech that can be used as a subjective complement are noun/pronoun(predicate nominative) or adjective(predicate adjective). The subjective complement describes the status or condition of the subject. The verbs that take subjective complements are: be-verbs (am, are, is, was, were, etc.), BP2 sensory verbs (feel, look, smell, sound, taste), and other state-of-being verbs(become, get, grow, turn, appear, remain, stay, prove, etc.) All these verbs are sometimes called **linking verbs**.

☞ *Note:* **BP2 Sensory verbs use adjectives as subjective complements, not adverbs** (Koreans may, at first, find it awkward to use adjectives in this case). I call these verbs BP2 sensory verbs to distinguish them from the sensory verbs used in BP5.

1.1.3 Basic Pattern 3 (BP3) – Complete Transitive Verbs

Verbs that use object

> **STRUCTURE: [SUBJECT] + [VERB] + [OBJECT]**
> **EX)[I] [LOVE] [YOU].**
> **[I] [SAID] [THAT YOU LOOKED DECENT].**

Complete transitive verbs are the verbs that need an object. Most verbs in English are transitive verbs.

Ex) want, say, like, hit, kill, touch, strengthen, etc.

The parts of speech that can be used as an object are noun/pronoun.

1.1.4 Basic Pattern 4 (BP4) – "Give" Verbs

> **STRUCTURE: [SUBJECT] + [VERB] + [INDIRECT OBJECT] + [DIRECT OBJECT]**
> **EX) [SHE] [GAVE] [ME] [A BOOK].**

"Give" verbs are the verbs that use an indirect object and a direct object.

Ex) give, bring, award, ask, tell, buy, grant, lend, offer, send, etc.

An indirect object is the person to whom or the thing to which the direct object is given, brought, awarded, asked, etc. A direct object is the person or thing that is given to the indirect object.

BP4 can be transformed into BP3 with a preposition.

Ex) "She gave a book to me."

1.1.5 Basic Pattern 5 (BP5) – Incomplete Transitive Verbs

STRUCTURE: [SUBJECT] + [VERB] + [OBJECT] + [OBJECTIVE COMPLEMENT]
EX) [GOD] [LET] [JESUS] [TAKE UP{THE CROSS}]

Incomplete transitive verbs are verbs that use an object and an objective complement.

Ex) make, have, let, get, help, see, watch, hear, feel, etc.

These verbs can be used as perfect transitive verbs depending on what you are trying to say. If the verb takes the object and its action or status as a whole, these verbs can act as incomplete transitive verbs. Most incomplete transitive verbs are either causatives (that cause somebody or something to do or to be done) or BP5 sensory verbs (as compared with BP2 sensory verbs).

Ex 1)   I want you. (BP3) => I want you to come. (BP5)

My father got me. (BP3) => My father got me to go to work. (BP5)

I saw my aunt. (BP3) => I saw my aunt smile. (BP5)

The parts of speech that can be used as an objective complement are verb, noun/pronoun, and adjective.

Ex 2)   My female friends helped me get a decent girlfriend. (verb)

I called him a bluffer. (noun)

The thug saw his boss approaching him with a gun in his hand. (adjective)

A verb can be used as a main verb in any two or more of these patterns. For example, as was explained in this chapter, a verb *sing* can be used as a complete intransitive verb or a complete transitive and another verb *feel* can be used as an incomplete intransitive verb or a complete transitive or even an incomplete transitive verb.

5 Basic Patterns	Structure
1: complete intransitive	Subject+Verb
2: incomplete intransitive	Subject+Verb+Subjective Complement
3: complete transitive	Subject+Verb+Object
4: "give" verb	Subject+Verb+Indirect Object+DirectObject
5: incomplete transitive	Subject+Verb+Object+Objective Complement

1.2 Parts of Speech

Another important concept is part of speech. There are **verbs, pronouns, nouns, adjectives, prepositions, conjunctions, adverbs,** and **interjections.** As you could see from the five basic patterns explained above, the **essential parts of speech** that are used to construct these basic patterns are:

- Noun/Pronoun, which can be used as the subject, the subjective complement or the object or the objective complement.

- Verb, which can be used as the simple predicate (or simply verb) or the objective complement.

- Adjective, which can be used as the subjective complement or the objective complement.

Then are the other parts of speech, such as adverbs, unimportant? No, it doesn't mean that they are unimportant; it means that you don't have to have them to make a whole and complete sentence whereas nouns/pronouns, verbs and adjectives are essential for a complete sentence depending on the patterns you use. The rest are used to make the sentence more elaborate and detailed. All of them are modifiers. And the appropriate and sophisticated use of these other parts of speech adequately inserted into these basic patterns will show whether the writer is proficient in English or not. One might always be grammatically correct and still not proficient in English if he or she cannot make the best use of these other parts of speech. Each of these parts of speech will be studied in detail in the following chapters.

☞ *Note:* Many English words can be used as multiple parts of speech.

> Ex 1) *Before I start on specific parts of speech, I have to explain this.* (before is used as a conjunction)
>
> *Before the exposition on parts of speech, I explained the five basic patterns.* (before is used as a preposition)
>
> *I had to explain this before.* (before is used as an adverb)

So, you have to determine a word's part of speech by examining its syntactic function, not simply by its form.

1.3   Chapter Exam on Basics

Indicate to which basic pattern the following sentences belong and put parentheses around the essential components of the basic pattern and indicate what they are (i.e., subject, verb, direct object, indirect object, subjective complement, objective complement). Also put a bracket around the clauses in the sentence and indicate what they are (whether independent or subordinate clause).

1. When the girl came to the U.S.A., she looked unbelievably vivacious according to what most of the people who knew her said.

2. If I saw you again, I would have you come and live with me for the rest of your life in my stunningly fabulous house custom-made for you.

3. I know that I will never be thirsty anymore because of the ever-flowing fountain of your love.

4. Could you please bring me that tasty fruit that you picked in the orchard?

5. In the middle of the Korean War when my whole family had to move all the way to Pusan where there was nobody who was nice enough to help us, our parents stood alone in that unfamiliar territory.

Find all grammar errors and correct them most efficiently (with minimal change). The following sentences may contain one, multiple, or no error(s).

6. All dishes in this restaurant tasted unbelievably badly and everybody who ate there felt very uncomfortably.

2 Verb

The verb is the most important and complex part of speech in English language as it is in most other languages. Most learners of English have a particularly hard time using verbs correctly. In this chapter, let us extensively study all the important usages of verbs and exceptions to the general rules summarized in the previous chapter.

2.1 Basics

2.1.1 Main Verb

When we compose a sentence, the most important thing is to make sure that there is at least one main verb in that sentence.
Whatever the type of a sentence (simple, complex, compound, or compound complex) you want to compose, you have to have at least one main verb (the verb in the independent clause) so that the sentence can become complete.

Ex 1) The Board of Directors of Exxon has decided to open new offices in Asian countries where Shell dominates the market nowadays.

Here, *decided* is the main verb; however, *dominates* is not, because it is a verb in a subordinate clause. In a complex sentence, there is only one main verb, and in compound or compound complex sentences, there are two or more main verbs.

Q1: Correct the following sentence.

The titans described in the myth written a long time ago when people believed in many gods worshipped in Greece and its surrounding countries.

This type of grammatical errors is called **Sentence Fragments** (or **missing main verbs**).

Another very important type of error related to the main verb is called the **Run-On Sentence** in which two independent clauses are not properly connected. You can properly connect two independent clauses:

- **by a coordinating conjunction** such as *but, or, yet, for, and, nor,* and *so* (**BOYFANS**)

- **by a subordinating conjunction** such as *after, before, because, since, when,* etc.

- **by a semicolon** when they are closely related (often with an appropriate conjunctive adverbs such as *therefore, however, consequently,* etc.). Refer to 8.1.4 for more details.

- **by a colon** when the second clause provides an explanation of the first clause.

These two kinds of grammatical errors are considered very serious mistakes, so you should avoid them in any formal writing even though in some literary and less formal writings, fragmented sentences are often used upon the author's discretion when the main verb is omitted because it is obvious.

> *Q2: Correct the following sentence.*
>
> *The greatest thing that happened to me is my wife, she is the most adorable and lovely woman people can't stop wanting to be near her.*

2.1.2 Verbs with Irregular Past Forms

Most of the verbs change to the past and the past participle forms by having –d or –ed attached, but a lot of very commonly used verbs change their forms irregularly. Here are some of the examples arranged in the sequence of present, past, and past participle:

Am/Is/Are	was/were	been
Become	became	become
Bite	bit	bitten
Break	broke	broken
Draw	drew	drawn
Drink	drank	drunk
Fly	flew	flown
Ride	rode	ridden
Shrink	shrank	shrunk
Swear	swore	sworn
Throw	threw	thrown
Weave	wove	woven
Withdraw	withdrew	withdrawn

There are hundreds of these irregular verbs, but as you can see from the list above, there is regularity even across some of these irregular verbs as to how their forms change. However, it may be more efficient and practical for some of you to repeat aloud the verb, its past form, and its past participle until you feel comfortable and confident with them, whenever you meet an irregular verb. When you accumulate your vocabulary, make sure that you identify these irregular verbs and memorize their irregular past and past participle forms.

Q: Correct the following sentence(s).

When the woman finded out that she had no cash in her pocket, she gone to the ATM and withdrawed five hundred dollars while I tried to find my friend who worn a red hat.

2.1.3 Auxiliary Verbs

There are verbs that help or modify other verbs. These so-called auxiliary verbs are sometimes called helping verbs. There are four kinds of auxiliary verbs.

- Modals: modals such as *can/could, may/might, shall/should, will/ would, must,* etc. have particular rules in their usages and help other verbs by giving various additional meanings which depend on how they are used in different contexts. Modals are extensively covered in Modal (Section 2.5)

- Be-Verbs: *be*-verbs (*am, is, are, was, were, been*) are used in progressive tense, covered in next section on tense and in passive voice, covered in section 2.3.

- Have-verbs: *have*-verbs (*have, has, had*) are used in perfect tenses and are covered in the next section.

- Do-verbs: *do*-verbs (*do, does, did*) are used to make a general question without any additional meaning, or to emphasize the verb

  Ex 1) She does need that title. (emphasis)

  ☞ **Note**: *Do*-verbs used as auxiliary verbs are followed by **the base form of a verb/the base-form verb** (also called the dictionary form of a verb, the verb word, the infinitival form, or the citation form, which has no –s attached).

☞ __*Note*__: Except the modals, the other auxiliary verbs can be used as main verbs and don't need other verb or verb-related word (or secondary verb explained in section 2.4) after them. However, modals are always used as auxiliary verbs and cannot be followed by other forms of verbs than the base forms.

These auxiliary verbs can be combined as long as they follow the syntactic rules required by the other auxiliary verbs used together. You will learn much about the syntactic rules that govern the formation of sentences containing complex verbs as you go along and analyze many example sentences.

Q: Correct the following sentence(s).

Because my dream do requires great interpersonal relationships, I would liked to work in that company, and my parents will are proud of me.

2.2 Tense

English has relatively clear distinctions of time and duration of action or state. Tense is a change of verb form used to express these distinctions. Let us briefly study basic tenses before proceeding into more complicated ones.

2.2.1 Simple Tenses

There are three kinds of simple tenses: past, present, and future. You simply use the past-form verbs for the past tense; you use present-form verbs for the present tense with proper inflections of the verb forms depending on whether the subject is singular or plural (i.e. if the subject of the present tense verb is singular, you use a singular verb which usually has –s or –es attached to the base form); and, finally, you use *will + verb word (base-form verb)* or *be-verb + going + to + base-form verb* for the future tense.

> *Ex 1)   The magnitude of the earthquake in L.A. <u>broke</u> all previous records in California.* (simple past tense)

> *Ex 2)   The <u>man</u> in front of the limousines that are as long as buses <u>has</u> more than one billion dollars.* (simple present tense)

Here, *has* instead of *have* is used because the **ultimate** (the simple) subject, *man*, is singular.

> *Ex 3)* She _will_ _call_ him the day after tomorrow
> She _is going to_ _call_ him the day after tomorrow. (simple future tense)

> **Q: Correct the following sentence(s).**
>
> *The world will be going to collapse in a century if the situation do not change in a positive direction.*

2.2.2 Progressive Tenses (Be-verb + Present Participle)

When you want to express an ongoing activity or state, you use progressive tenses. In a parallel with the simple tenses, progressive tenses have three kinds: past progressive, present progressive, and future progressive. The structure of a progressive tense is *be-verb + present participle* (the ~*ing* form). You conjugate the be-verb to show the differences in time.

> *Ex 1)* My nephew _was_ _crying_ without a pause. (past progressive tense)
>
> *Ex 2)* My niece _is_ _playing_ the cello in her room. (present progressive tense)
>
> *Ex 3)* My granddaughter _will_ _be_ _attending_ your wedding. (future progressive tense)

2.2.3 Perfect Tenses (Have/Has/Had/Will have + Past Participle)

Perfect tenses also have three kinds: past perfect (*had* + *p.p.*), present perfect (*have/has* + *p.p.*) and future perfect (*will* + *have* + *p.p.*). Because, unlike the other tenses, the cases or meanings in which present perfect, past perfect, and future perfect tenses are used are very different, let us consider these separately.

2.2.3.1 Present Perfect (Have/Has + Past Participle)

Let's consider the present perfect tense first. You use the present perfect tense for the following cases:

1. When the activity or state is extended over a period of time until now or when it repeats during that time period.

    Ex 1) *Esther has attended this kindergarten since she became five years old.*

    Ex 2) *Esther has attended this kindergarten for five years.*

    Ex 3) *Esther has received five A's so far this academic year.*

    For this usage of perfect tenses, you often use *since, for, over, so far* as the examples above show. **Whenever you see [for]+[duration such as *five years* and *two hours*] or [since]+[time in the past or action in the past], you have to use a perfect tense in the independent clause.**

2. When the exact time of the activity or event is not important and you simply want to express whether that activity or event has happened in the past.

    Ex 4) *The research fellows have never seen such a laboratory in their lives.*

    Ex 5) *Have you ever traveled outside your own country?*

    Ex 6) *Our congregation hasn't come to a consensus yet.*

    For this usage of perfect tenses, you often use *ever, never, yet, already, just, still,* etc., as the examples above show.

> *Q: Correct the following sentence(s).*
>
> *Although human beings were in various kinds of wars since the beginning of the world, there was no reported war for the past two years.*

2.2.3.2 Past Perfect (Had + Past Participle)

The past perfect tense is used when you want to express an activity or event that was completed before another activity or event in the past.

Ex 1) *King Kong had been considered the greatest sci-fi movie before E.T. came out.*

When the sequence of time is very obvious by the use of *before* or *after*, simple past is, informally, often used instead of past perfect.

Ex 2)   *After everybody (had) left, the pastor got out of the burning house.*

However, it is recommended that you use the past perfect tense even in this case when you are writing formally.

Error 1) *By December, 1900, most people worked part-time in that city.*

Error 2) *Students argued with the teachers for five hours before the principal finally intervened.*

When you have [by] + [a specific time in the past] or [for] + [a specific time period] or [since] + [a time in the past] to indicate an activity or state that had been going on until a certain point in the past, you have to use a past perfect tense in the main clause.

Corr 1) *By December, 1900, most people had worked part-time in that city.*

Corr 2) *Students had argued with the teachers for five hours before the principal finally intervened.*

Q: Correct the following sentence(s).

The gas station earned millions of dollars by the time a bigger company took over. Before the takeover, the owner lived a luxurious life.

2.2.3.3 Future Perfect (Will + Have + Past Participle)

The future perfect tense is used when you want to express a prediction for a future activity or event by a certain point in the future.

Ex)   *All of the students who study with and follow the instructions of the "Optimal English" series will have accumulated all the essential knowledge about English by the third year.*

Because the future perfect predicts that some activity or event will have happened or will not have happened by some future time, adverbial phrases led by *by* are often used.

Q: Correct the following sentence(s).

Their race will have at least 10 Nobel Prize winners in the field of Literature by 2100.

Q: Correct the following sentence(s).

1. *The kids will complete this program about self-control by next month.*
2. *The song is one of the greatest hits since it was aired on TV.*
3. *By the time I finished my duty, my boss completed his job.*

2.2.4 Perfect Progressive Tenses (Have/Has/Had + Been + Present Participle)

The perfect progressive tenses are used when you want to express and emphasize that an activity or event is extended over a period of time and is being continued. Like other tenses, you have past, present, and future perfect progressive tenses. The usages and meanings are parallel with those in the perfect tenses. The following examples show past perfect progressive, present perfect progressive, and future perfect progressive, respectively.

Ex 1) *Educators had been studying different school systems for three years by the time (or when)the government collected enough data.*

Ex 2) *Educators have been studying different school systems for five years*

Ex 3) *Educators will have been studying different school systems for more than three years by the end of this decade.*

2.2.5 Action Immediately Following Another Action

There are several ways to express an action that follows immediately after another action. Pay attention to which tenses are used for each and how the actions are linked.

- **The moment:**

  Ex 1) *The moment you see him, call me.*

- **As soon as:**

  Ex 2) *As soon as I graduated from my school, I enlisted in the Navy.*

  Ex 3) *As soon as I get a job, I will get out of this house.*

- **No sooner ~ than ~:**

  Ex 4) Her law firm had no sooner closed down than she left the firm.

  Ex 5) No sooner had her law firm closed down than she left the firm.

Notice the **inversion** of the word order in the second example; the auxiliary verb *had* comes before the subject, *her law firm*, because the negative adverbial phrase *no sooner* comes first and is emphasized. This is called **inversion** in a grammatical terminology, and this concept will be treated later in detail (refer to section 6.6 Inversion (Emphasis of Adverbs).

- **Hardly/Scarcely ~ when ~:**

  Ex 6) My laptop computer had hardly/scarcely started when the power went out.

  Ex 7) Hardly/scarcely had my laptop computer started when the power went out.

Again, inversion is used in the second example.

Q: Correct the following sentence(s).

Saudi Arabia no sooner found a vast oil field when the price of oil plummeted.

2.2.6 Special Tense-Agreement

Error 1) When they will watch the lachrymose Korean drama, they (will) cry.

You cannot use future tense in clauses starting with *when* or *if*.

Corr 1) When they watch the lachrymose Korean drama, they (will) cry.

Ex 1) Whenever she watches the lachrymose Korean drama, she cries.

When you use *whenever* and present tense in its clause, you have to use present tense in the main clause, not future tense because you are talking about a current habit; however, in a casual speech, you can use future tense.

Error 2) <u>When</u> she <u>watched</u> the hilarious drama, she <u>laughs</u> a lot.

The tense in the main clause must agree with the tense of the clause starting with *when*, except for cases shown in Ex 6 of 2.2.5 or in Ex 1 of 2.2.4.

Corr 2) <u>When</u> she <u>watched</u> the hilarious drama, she <u>laughed</u> a lot.

> *Q: Correct the following sentence(s).*
>
> *I have been lean and fit when I started to nurse my child.*

2.3 Passive Voice

Passive voice is the grammatical structure in which the agent receiving the action, rather than the doer of the action, comes in the subject's place. **In modern English, in which the economy of language is very important, passive voice is avoided as much as possible when using active voice doesn't change the meaning of the sentence and when using active voice is shorter and clearer to understand. However, there are cases in which the use of passive voice is often preferred.**

2.3.1 Basic Structure

> *Ex)* *All of the citizens of the empire <u>respected</u> the reputed scholar.*
>
> *=> The reputed scholar <u>was</u> <u>respected</u> <u>by</u> all of the citizens of the empire.*

As the example shows, in the passive voice, the subject, *the reputed scholar*, receives respect rather than gives respect. The basic form of passive voice is as follows:

[Subject(or the agent receiving the action)] + [Be-verb] + [past participle of a transitive verb] + {[prepositions such as *by* or *with, at, about, in,* etc.] + [the agent giving the action]}

The parts in {} can be omitted when they are obvious or not important. You can also have other auxiliary verbs (helping verbs) such as modals or *have/do/be–verbs* between the subject and the *be-verb*.

2.3.2 Active Voice that Has a Passive Meaning

- There are some verbs that can have a passive meaning in certain cases: *read, sell, wash*, etc.

> Ex 1) *The condominiums in that subdivision are <u>selling</u> <u>like crazy</u> nowadays.*

☞ *<u>Note</u>*: To be used in this way, these verbs normally require a following adverbial phrase that modifies them.

> *Error 1) This book <u>reads</u>.*
> *Corr 1) This book <u>reads</u> <u>extremely easily.</u>*

- When an infinitive comes after an adjective and the subject is the agent receiving the action, you can simply use the active form in the infinitive.

> Ex 2) *<u>The turquoise dress</u> is <u>luxurious</u> <u>to wear.</u>*

- When infinitives are used to describe a task to be done and the subject of the sentence is a person doing the task, you simply use the active form in the infinitives.

> Ex 3) *<u>She</u> has <u>a big problem</u> <u>to take care of.</u>*
> This is preferred to
> *She has a big problem <u>to be taken care of</u>.*

- Gerunds coming after the verbs like *need, want, require* and *deserve* have passive meanings.

> Ex 4) *My car <u>needs</u> <u>repairing</u>.*
> *= My car <u>needs</u> <u>to be repaired</u>.*

Q: Correct the following sentence(s).

My copying machine is extremely easy to be used.

2.3.3 Passive Voice Using Prepositions Other than *By*

Most of the passive voice forms use the preposition *by* in front of the agent; however, there are some verbs(or p.p.'s to be more precise) that use other prepositions.

- **With:** *acquainted, amused, associated, bored, concerned, covered, crowded, delighted, disappointed, dissatisfied, equipped, filled, gratified, pleased, satisfied, preoccupied, married, etc.*

  Ex 1)   The secretary of defense <u>was</u> totally <u>satisfied with</u> the result of the nuclear test.

- **At (*or* By):** *alarmed, amazed, astonished, astounded, shocked, surprised, etc.*

  Ex 2)   The cabinet members <u>were</u> devastatingly <u>shocked at</u> the horrible news.

- **About:** *concerned, worried, troubled, excited, etc.*

  Ex 3)   The children <u>were</u> <u>worried about</u> their parents' leaving them.

- **In:** *absorbed, caught, engaged*(which, in this usage, means *occupied*), *engrossed, interested, etc.*

  Ex 4)   The dean had <u>been absorbed in</u> the treatise written by an undergraduate student.

There are of course other prepositions used in passive voice: **of** (after p.p.'s like *composed, frightened, scared, terrified, made* (when there is no chemical change), etc.), **to** (after *accustomed, addicted, betrothed, engaged*(which means *betrothed*), *committed, devoted, dedicated, married, opposed,* etc.), **from** (after *derived, exhausted, made* (when there is a chemical change), etc.). These are rather like idioms in the sense that you have to practice these until you know them by heart. As you can see, when these verbs are used passively, the subject is, most of the time, a human or an animate being.

☞ *Note*: Some of these passive phrases change their meanings depending on which preposition is used with them.

Ex 5)   I am <u>concerned about</u> you. (meaning "worried about")

Ex 6)   The project is <u>concerned with</u> racism. (meaning "related to" or "involved in")

☞ _Note_: The preposition "_to_" deserves special attention. Because the _to_ that follows _accustomed, addicted, married,_ or _opposed_ is a **preposition** rather than the infinitival _to_, you have to use a gerund form rather than a base-form verb after it (because gerunds, not infinitives, are used as the object of prepositions). **Distinguishing the two different types of "to" is very important.**

> _Q: Correct the following sentence(s)._
>
> _When my granddaughter was engrossed with science in high school, I, as a scientist, was very satisfied about her endeavor._

2.4 Secondary Verbs

Secondary verbs are words that are derived from verbs but are used as different parts of speech. In that sense, secondary verbs are technically not verbs but rather nouns, adjectives, or adverbs. Secondary verbs include the infinitives, the gerunds, and the participles.

2.4.1 Infinitive

There are two kinds of infinitives.

- Base infinitives: These have the same form as the base-form verbs. They are typically used as nouns and as objective complements in the basic pattern 5 shown below.

  Ex 1)   Michael heard his mom come down from upstairs.

  Ex 2)   My in-laws made me quit smoking for my wife's sake.

  In many other grammar books, these base infinitives are not adequately dealt with and the following _to_-infinitives conventionally represent the infinitives. Do not be confused by all these somewhat nonessential terms.

- To-infinitives: These are formed by "_to_" plus the base-form verbs. These are used as nouns, adjectives, or adverbs.

  Ex 3)   To die is to gain. (both are used as nouns, the first in the subject's place and the second in the subjective complement's place)

  Ex 4)   I want to keep helping you to the end. (used as a noun in the object's place)

> *Ex 5)*   *There are things <u>to remember</u> and things <u>to forget</u> in*
> *our lives.* (these to-infinitives are used as adjectives
> that modify the nouns in front of them)
>
> *Ex 6)*   *<u>To find</u> out what the truth is, many philosophers have*
> *spent their whole lives delving into the laws of life.*
> (here, the to-infinitive is used as an adverb)

**Q: Indicate which parts of speech the following underlined infinitives
are used as.**

*The purpose of my life is <u>to love and help</u> others, and <u>to do</u> that
consistently, I know there must be someone <u>to believe in.</u>*

> *Ex 7)*   *The money received from the government was*
> *enough <u>for</u> <u>him</u> <u>to prepare</u> for his wedding.*
>
> *Ex 8)*   *It was really kind <u>of</u> <u>her</u> <u>to call</u> him.*

To indicate the subject of the infinitive (when it is not obvious),
you usually use [*for*] + [the subject of the infinitive (an objective
case pronoun, if it is a pronoun)] + [infinitive].
However, sometimes, you use *of* (as in Ex 8), or sometimes you
don't use any preposition (as in some BP 5 structures).

2.4.2 Gerund

Gerunds are formed by attaching *–ing* to verbs. They have the same
forms as present participles, but gerunds are used as nouns whereas
present participles are used as adjectives or adverbs. In other words,
gerunds must come in noun's place.

> *Ex 1)*   *<u>Walking</u> along the street is often fun.* (gerund)
>
> *Ex 2)*   *<u>Walking</u> along the street, I came across the person I was*
> *searching for my entire life.* (participle)

In the first example, the word, "*walking*," is a gerund because it is used
as a noun. In the second sentence, it is a present participle because it is
not in the noun's place. It just leads an adjective or adverbial phrase.
This special adverbial or adjectival phrase is called participial phrase.

Q: Indicate whether the underlined words are gerund or present participle.

Pouring hot tea into a stunning cup, the lady finally stopped talking with the most exciting person she has ever met in her entire banking career in which a lot of her hiring and firing numerous people took place.

Ex 3)   *I will never be able to understand his living like a recluse with so many things in his brain to share with the world.*

Ex 4)   *When I met the barbarians, my uncle reminded me of their killing my kinsmen brutally and relentlessly.*

Living in Ex 3 is a gerund used as the object of the verb *understand*, and *killing* in Ex 4 is a gerund used as the object of preposition *of*. You can use only gerunds, not infinitives, as the objects of prepositions. **To indicate the subject of a gerund, you have to use a possessive noun or pronoun instead of an objective noun or pronoun.** You have to be able to distinguish a gerund from a present participle in order not to make this mistake.

☞ *Note*: The above concept does not mean that you cannot have an objective case before ~ing form because a present participle may be used to modify the noun/pronoun used as an object of a verb or a preposition.

Ex 5)   *My teacher reminded me of my father teaching me how to read.*

The object of the preposition *of* in the above sentence is *my father*, not his action *teaching*. The word *teaching* used here is a present participle modifying *my father*. Let's contrast this with the following sentence.

Ex 6)   *My teacher's teaching reminded me of my father's teaching me how to read.*

However, here, the object of the preposition *of* is *teaching*, which is gerund, not *my father's*. **When the action is the intended object of a verb or a preposition (i.e., the gerund is the object), you must avoid a common error of using an objective case instead of a possessive case in front of a gerund.**

Q: Correct the following sentence(s).

At the end of the battle in which my grandfather fought as the general, the soldiers were horrified at him leaving innocent infants in the battlefield.

2.4.3 Participle

There are two kinds of participles: present participle and past participle.

- Present participle: This is formed by attaching –ing to the base form of a verb. There are, as usual, slight spelling irregularities for this like *dying* from *die*, *hitting* from *hit*, etc.

- Past participle: This is the past participle as we studied in 2.1.2 Participles are used mostly as adjectives and sometimes as adverbs when used in participial phrase.

Ex 1)   <u>Wanted</u> by most international intelligence agencies, the killer completely hid himself from public exposure.

Ex 2)   I cannot drink this <u>contaminated</u> water.

Ex 3)   For the record, <u>jumping</u> jacks is the fundamental exercise for this kind of sport.

The first example shows a past participle used as an adverb in an adverbial phrase (it could also be considered an adjective modifying the subject of the main clause). In the second and third examples, the past and the present participles are used as adjectives that describe the nouns after them.

Q: Indicate which parts of speech the underlined words are used as.

<u>Confronted</u> with the <u>continuing</u> series of economically detrimental events, the <u>policy-making</u> board of directors will have to postpone <u>increasing</u> the salary of more than 50 percent of the <u>employed</u> personnel so that they don't have to penalize other <u>hard-working</u> people who were <u>hired</u> a long time ago.

2.4.4 Participial Phrase

Participial Phrases need some special treatment. Participial phrases are adverbial or adjectival phrases led by either a present participle or a past participle. These can be used when the omitted subject of the participle is the same as the subject of the main clause. The conjunctions can be omitted if they are obvious like *as, when, because,* etc.

> *Ex 1)* *Because he had been very sick because of the flu, he soon became exhausted.*
> *=> Being very sick because of the flu, he soon became exhausted.*
>
> *Ex 2)* *When my dog was hit by a car on the small street, she lost one of her legs.*
> *=> Hit by a car on the small street, my dog lost one of her legs.*

When the conjunctions are not general or if you want to clarify the meaning, you have to specify them.

> *Ex 3)* *While the professor stayed at the university, he taught thousands of Ph. D. students.*
> *=>While staying at the university, he taught thousands of Ph. D. students.*

This type of construction is sometimes called an elliptical clause because the obvious subject is not stated within that dependent clause.

When you want to indicate in the participial phrase an action in the earlier time, you use *having + p.p.*

> *Ex 4)* *Because I ran very hard, now I am totally exhausted.*
> *=> Having run very hard, now I am totally exhausted.*

2.4.5 Dangling Participial/Gerund/Infinitive Phrases

For the sake of efficiency, using participial phrases are recommended whenever it doesn't change the meaning.

However, you have to be very careful not to use a dangling participial phrase. Dangling participial phrases occur when the omitted (or implied) subject of the participle in a participial phrase differs from the subject of the main clause.

Error 1) <u>*Having exercised*</u> *for more than one hour,* <u>*his muscles*</u> *became stupendously pumped up.*

This sentence is ungrammatical because the omitted subject of "exercising" is a person, not muscles. So you should change the sentence into one of the following.

Corr 1A) <u>*Having exercised*</u> *for more than one hour,* <u>*he*</u> *pumped up his muscles stupendously.*

Corr 1B) <u>*After he had exercised*</u> *for more than one hour,* <u>*his muscles*</u> *became stupendously pumped up.*

In other words, you either match the subject of the main clause with the omitted subject of the participle or use a clause instead of a participial phrase.

☞ ***Note***: Dangling participial phrase is the most common dangling-modifier problem; however, there are also **dangling elliptical clauses, dangling gerund phrases, and dangling infinitive phrases.**

Error 2) *When* <u>*offered*</u> *a one-trillion-dollar fund,* <u>*a new, transparent fund-managing policy*</u> *had to be made.* (a dangling elliptical clause)

Here the unstated subject of the subordinate clause has to be a person; thus, you have to change the subject of the main clause to a person if you want to have an elliptical adverbial clause.

Corr 2) *When* <u>*offered*</u> *a one-trillion-dollar fund,* <u>*you*</u> *have to make a new, transparent fund-managing policy.*

Error 3) <u>*By investing*</u> *in a diversified portfolio,* <u>*your asset*</u> *can be secured.* (dangling gerund phrase error)

This is a typical dangling gerund error in which the omitted subject of the gerund investing, which must be a person, is not used as the subject of the main clause.

Corr 3) <u>*By investing*</u> *in a diversified portfolio,* <u>*you*</u> *can secure your asset.*

Error 4) <u>*To amass*</u> *wealth optimally,* <u>*your asset*</u> *must be redistributed.* (dangling infinitive phrase error)

Again, only a person can amass wealth; thus, a person should be the subject of the main clause.

Corr 4) *To amass wealth optimally, you must redistribute your asset.*

2.5 Modal

Modals are used with other verbs to give additional meanings to those verbs. Some of the most important fundamental grammatical rules in using modals are

1) **After the modal, only the base form of a verb is used.**
2) **When negating the modal, you have to attach the negative words such as not and never right after the modal.**

Let us first study the most commonly used modals and then the modal-related idioms. There could be many different usages of these modals other than what I list in the following, but these usages are most widely used and, for most cases, sufficient.

2.5.1 Can/Could

Can can give additional meanings of ability, possibility or permission.

Could can give additional meanings of ability in the past, possibility or permission.

Ex 1) *I can (= am able to) design an exquisite model house.*
(present ability)
I could (= was able to) lift this weight two years ago.
(past ability)

Ex 2) *It can happen! It could happen!* (present possibility)

Ex 3) *Can/Could we register for the class right now?* (permission)

When you want to express past possibility, you have to combine *can/could* with *have + p.p.* (past participle).

Ex 4) *We cannot say that the actress is a liar because she can/could have been really sick.* ("hindsight" possibility of a past event; in this case, could is more widely used.)

Can and *could* are almost equivalent in meaning and use, but *could* usually expresses a slightly lower probability and higher politeness than *can*.

2.5.2 May/Might

May can give additional meanings of present probability or permission.

Might gives an additional meaning of present probability, probability from the point of view of the past, or permission.

> *Ex 1)*   *What the senator is proclaiming may/might be important to our agenda.* (present probability)
>
> *Ex 2)*   *I told my aunt that I might visit her in the spring.* (probability from the point of view of the past)
>
> *Ex 3)*   *May/Might I introduce my fiancée?* (permission)

When you want to express the probability of a past event from the point of view of the present, you have to combine *may/might* with *have* + *p.p.* (past participle).

> *Ex 4)*   *According to some historians, the start of the last tribulation period may/might have already arrived several years ago.* (probability of a past event from the point of view of the present)

May and *might* are almost equivalent in meaning and use but *might* usually expresses a slightly lower probability and higher politeness than *may*.

2.5.3 Will/Would

Will gives an additional meaning of futurity with certainty.

> *Ex 1)*   *Immigrants will stop coming into our country unless our government does something about this prevalent problem of discrimination against foreigners.* (future)

Would can give additional meanings of futurity from the point of view of the past, habitual action, or more politeness.

Ex 2)   *The principal <u>said</u> that she <u>would</u> enhance the quality of the boarding school.* (futurity in the point of view of the past)

Ex 3)   *When my children <u>were</u> young, they <u>would</u> take a nap right after lunch.* (habitual action of the past)

Ex 4)   *<u>Would</u> you (please) speak more loudly?* (more politeness as compared to "Will you speak more loudly")

Will + *have* + *p.p.* is used in future perfect (refer to 2.2.3.3) and *Would* + *have* + *p.p.* is used in Subjunctive Past Perfect (refer to 2.7.2.2)

2.5.4 Shall/Should

Shall can give additional meanings of simple futurity in the first person or obligation in the second or third person or stipulations in laws.

Ex 1)   *I <u>shall</u> call him "the boss."* (simple futurity in the first person)

Ex 2)   *You <u>shall</u> listen to your father.* (obligation in the second person)

Ex 3)   *The earnest money deposit <u>shall</u> be $1000.* (stipulation in legal documents)

Nowadays, *will* often replaces shall in most usages except in legal documents.

Should can give additional meanings of obligation or prediction.

Ex 4)   *The instructors <u>should</u> follow the rules of the academy.* (obligation)

Ex 5)   *The letter <u>should</u> be here very soon.* (prediction)

When you want to express an obligation or necessity in the past, you have to combine *should* with *have* + *p.p.* (past participle).

Ex 5)   *I <u>should</u> have told you what kind of person he was.* (obligation in the past that was regrettably not met)

2.5.5 Must

Must adds the meanings of obligation or logical conclusion with almost 100% certainty.

Ex 1)   *The stockholders <u>must</u> claim their rights before it is too late.* (obligation)

Ex 1)   *That main guitarist __must__ be Eric Clapton.* (logical conclusion about the present event)

How do we know which meaning of *must* is used in various sentences? It is sad that there is no definite answer, but *must* usually has the meaning of obligation if you have an action verb after *must* and the meaning of logical conclusion if you have a be-verb after *must*. Nevertheless, its meaning should be derived out of the whole context of the passage or conversation. Look at the following example.

Ex 3)   *You __must__ call often.*

Depending on what the context was, the above sentence could mean "You have to call often" or "It must be the case that you call often."

Because it is impossible to generalize some of these English grammatical rules, you can truly master English and its grammar only by reading a lot of well-written writings while applying and reviewing the knowledge you gained from this book.

When you are making a logical conclusion about the event in the past, you have to combine *must* with *have + p.p.* (past participle).

Ex 4)   *That main guitarist __must__ __have__ __been__ Eric Clapton.*
          (logical conclusion about a past event)

Q: Correct the following sentence(s).

According to the report, the majority of the refugees might already starve to death a week ago; it is likely that the food supply must be intercepted by the rebels when it was being delivered to the refugees .

2.5.6 Other Modals / Modal-Related Idioms

The following less commonly used modals and modal-related idioms are very similar to modals. Know clearly how and where to add negative adverbs (*not, never*, etc.) in the sentence and what kind of verb form you have to use after these idioms.

- **Need:** *Need* can be used as a modal or as a common verb.

    Ex 1)   *I __need__ __sleep__ now. I __need__ __not__ sleep now. I __need__ __to__ sleep. I __don't__ __need__ to sleep.*

- **Dare:** *Dare* can be used as a modal or as a common verb.

  > *Ex 2)*   *I <u>dare</u> <u>speak</u> to him. I <u>dare</u> <u>not</u> <u>speak</u> to him like that. I <u>dared</u> <u>to talk</u> to him. I <u>did</u> <u>not</u> <u>dare</u> <u>to talk</u> to him.*

- **Had better:** advisability on a future action.

  > *Ex 3)*   *You <u>had better</u> take this pill.*
  > *You <u>had better</u> <u>not</u> take this pill.*

- **Would rather:** preference for oneself.

  > *Ex 4)*   (preference of a future action)
  > *I <u>would rather</u> attend a community college.*
  > *I <u>would rather</u> <u>not</u> attend a community college.*

  > *Ex 5)*   (preference of a past event from the present point of view)
  > *I <u>would rather</u> <u>have</u> <u>attended</u> a college.*
  > *I <u>would rather</u> <u>not</u> <u>have</u> <u>attended</u> a college.*

- **Would rather that:** preference for others.

  > *Ex 6)*   (preference of a future action)
  > *I <u>would rather</u> <u>that you</u> <u>attended</u> a community college.*
  > *I <u>would rather</u> <u>that you</u> <u>didn't</u> attend a community college.*

Notice that you use a past verb within the 'that' clause even if it means a future action.

  > *Ex 7)*   (preference of a past event from the present point of view)
  > *I <u>would rather</u> <u>that you</u> <u>had</u> <u>attended</u> a college.*
  > *I <u>would rather</u> <u>that you</u> <u>had</u> <u>not</u> <u>attended</u> a college.*
  > *college.*

You use past perfect tense in the the that clause in this case.

- **Ought to:** obligation, advisability, or logical expectation.

  > *Ex 8)*   *You <u>ought</u> <u>to</u> clean your filthy room.*
  > *You <u>ought</u> <u>not</u> <u>to</u> clean your filthy room.*
  > (some people prefer *ought not clean*)

- **Would you please:** polite request.

> *Ex 9) Would you please sing loudly?*
> *Would you please not sing loudly?*

- **Would you mind/Do you mind:** asking for an approval.

> *Ex 10) Would you mind/Do you mind closing the door for*
> *me?*
> *Would you mind/Do you mind not closing the door*
> *for me?*

You have to use a gerund after these phrases.

☞ *Note*: If you answer "yes" to the first question in the last example, you mean that you don't want to close the door, and if you answer "yes" to the second question, then you mean that you want to close the door. So when you want to be polite and allow the asker his/her request, you normally say "no" to these kinds of questions.

☞ *Note*: **Have to/had to** is used as a main verb, so unlike most of the modals/modal-related idioms above, you can use this after modals or even as infinitives. It indicates the obligatory nature and necessity of a present/past action.

> *Ex 11) The dropouts had to take the exam to be eligible to apply to*
> *that institution.*

The dropouts didn't have to take the exam to be eligible to apply to that institution.

Q: Correct the following sentence(s).

The plaintiff would rather that I complete the documents, but I had not better complete them without my attorney.

2.6 Mood

There are three types of mood in English verbs: indicative mood, imperative mood, and subjunctive mood.

Ex 1) She loves her two sons very much. (indicative)

Ex 2) Love your neighbor as yourself. (imperative)

Ex 3) Her father and pastor suggested that she love her husband.
(subjunctive, in this case, subjunctive present)

Indicative mood is the most common mood that simply states or questions something. Imperative mood is used when you give an order. Subjunctive mood is used when you are not stating facts or simple conditions but rather expressing wish, want, assumption of contrary-to-fact conditions, or indirect command. The first two moods are very common and simple, but the subjunctive mood needs much explanation. In the next section, let us study conditionals and relevant subjunctive mood usages.

2.7 Conditionals (if/unless) and Subjunctive Mood

Conditionals are statements that involve *if* or *unless* (= *if ~ not~*). There are two kinds of conditionals: real or factual conditionals and unreal or contrary-to-fact conditionals. Factual conditionals express absolute and scientific results or probable and possible results whereas contrary-to-fact conditionals express improbable or impossible results. Some people call the use of the contrary-to-fact conditionals **subjunctive mood** even though, to be precise, subjunctive mood comprises much more than the contrary-to-fact conditionals.

The basic word order for conditionals is as follows:

[If/unless] + [subject] + [**verb**] + [,] + [main subject] + [**main verb**]

Now the important part that determines what kind of conditional the sentence belongs to is the form of the verb in the if clause and that of the verb in the main clause.

2.7.1 Factual Conditionals

> Ex 1)   *If this lethal virus starts to spread, those poor animals (will) die.* (scientific fact)

Because this is a scientific fact, you can use a present verb in the *if* clause and in the main clause (when you want to say that the result automatically follows). If you use *will* in the main clause, you are predicting with certainty that the said result will absolutely occur if not automatically.

> Ex 2)   *If you come to my house, (then) I will(shall, can, may, etc.) serve an authentic Korean dish to you.* (probable result)

The modals, *will/would, shall/should, can/could, may/might,* are used in the main clause, indicating different levels of probability of the result in a decreasing order. You may start the independent clause with *then.*

Ex 3)   Unless you are an idiot, you can't miss his intention.
= If you are not an idiot, you can't miss his intention.

You can always use *unless* to mean *if~ not ~*.

Ex 4)   If that imbecile <u>was</u> the hand behind all that mess, I <u>am going</u>
<u>to punish</u> him accordingly.

Even though this kind of usage is rare, it is possible to use past tense in the *if* clause to indicate uncertainty about a past event or action. Refer to the next section to compare this with subjunctive past.

2.7.2 Contrary-to-Fact Conditionals and Subjunctive Mood

Subjunctive means unusual change in verb forms that seems inconsistent with the general rules of subject-verb agreement or tense. Thus you will see some anomalous usages of verb forms in most of these subjunctive moods. There are subjunctive past, subjunctive past perfect, and subjunctive present.

2.7.2.1 Subjunctive Past

When you want to express hope or wish for something **that is probably not true or not going to happen**, you use subjunctive past.

Ex 1)   If they <u>studied</u> hard, they <u>would (or should, could, might) pass</u>
the exam. (improbable or contrary to the fact in the present)

= <u>Should</u> they <u>study</u> hard, they <u>would (or should, could, might)</u>
<u>pass</u> the exam. (inversion when if/unless is omitted; this usage,
however, is archaic)

≈ Because they don't study hard, they will not pass the exam.

The basic structure of subjunctive past is as follows:

[If] + [S] + [past verb/were/past form of a modal] …, [S] + [should/would/could/might (in the order of decreasing probability)]

Understand that even though a past verb is used in the if clause, it means the improbability of **the present action** in this case.

When you use a **be-verb** in an *if* clause, **you have to use *were* no matter what the subject is when you want to express the contrary-to-fact or impossible action or state of the present.** Because *were* after a third person singular noun/pronoun is the only unusual change of verb form from the past indicative mood, ***were*** can be considered the only true subjunctive past that clearly shows contrary-to-fact assumption.

> *Ex 2)*   If I <u>were</u> a bird, I <u>would fly</u> to you.
>   = <u>Were</u> I a bird, I <u>would fly</u> to you. (inversion when if/unless is omitted)

You can also use *modal + have + p.p.* for the main clause when subjunctive past is used in the *if* clause; however, the time of the action or the state in the main clause is clearly not present but past.

> *Ex 3)*   *If she <u>were</u> the current CEO, she <u>would</u> <u>have</u> <u>made</u> the inauguration speech <u>the day before yesterday.</u>*
>   *≈Because she <u>is not</u> the <u>current</u> CEO, she <u>didn't</u> make the inauguration speech <u>the day before yesterday.</u>*

Some of the other common usages that are related to subjunctive past are as follows:

- **Wish:**

> *Ex 4)*   *I <u>wish</u> <u>that</u> I <u>were</u> rich now. (≈ I want to be rich now though I am not.)*
>   *I <u>wished</u> that he <u>were</u> rich. (≈ I wanted him to be rich though he was not.)*
>   *I <u>wish</u> I <u>would</u> <u>fall</u> <u>asleep</u>. (≈ I hope that I will fall asleep.)* (This case is not really a subjunctive past)

- **As if/as though:**

> *Ex 5)*   *He <u>is talking</u> <u>as if</u> he <u>were</u> the winner. (≈ He is not the winner, but he is talking like the winner.)*
>   *He <u>talked</u> <u>as if / as though</u> he <u>were</u> the winner! (≈ He was not the winner, but he talked like the winner.)*
>   *He <u>talks</u> <u>as if / as though</u> he <u>would be</u> the winner! (≈ He talks, believing that he will be the winner.)* (Again, this is not really a subjunctive past)

In the subordinate clause, use subjunctive past to indicate your wish for the event at the same time of the "wishing" and *would + base-form verb* for the event that happens later from the main verb's point of view.

> **Q: Correct the following sentence(s).**
>
> *Was it the herd of sheep that destroyed our grass-rich field, we would find many footprints, and I actually wish that the shepherd was responsible for this, but it is obvious that he is not.*

2.7.2.2 Subjunctive Past Perfect

When you want to express hope or wish for something **that didn't happen or wasn't the case,** you use subjunctive past perfect.

Ex 1)   *If the agent <u>had known</u> about the collusion, he <u>would (or should, could, might)</u> <u>have sued</u> the other party*

       Or

       <u>Had</u> the agent <u>known</u> about the collusion, he <u>would (or should, could, might)</u> <u>have sued</u> the other party.
       (inversion when if/unless is omitted)

       ≈ *Because the agent did not know about the collusion, he did not sue the other party.*

The past perfect tense is used in the *if* clause, and [*should, would, could or might*, in the order of decreasing probability] + [*have*] + [*p. p.*] is used in the main clause.

You can also use *modal + base-form verb* for the main clause; however, the time of the action or the state in the main clause is clearly not past but present.

Ex 2)   *If my fiancé <u>had not</u> <u>called</u> my dad <u>the day before the wedding,</u> we <u>would</u> be happily married now.*

       ≈ *Because my fiancé <u>called</u> my dad <u>the day before the wedding</u>, we <u>are</u> <u>not</u> happily married <u>now</u>.*

Some of the other common usages are as follows:

- **Wish:**

> *Ex 3)*   *I <u>wish</u> <u>that</u> I <u>had</u> <u>met</u> him before! (≈ Though I didn't meet him before, I wish I had.)*
>
> *I <u>wished</u> <u>that</u> <u>you</u> <u>had</u> <u>participated</u> in that event. (≈Though you had not participated in that event, I wished you had.)*

- **As if/as though:**

> *Ex 5)*   *He talks <u>as if / as though</u> he <u>had been</u> the winner! (≈ Though he was not the winner, he talks as if he had been the winner.)*
>
> *He talked <u>as if / as though</u> he <u>had been</u> the winner. (≈ Though he had not been the winner, he talked as if he had been the winner.)*

You may replace *as if / as though* with *like* in a casual speech; however, formally, *like* is a preposition, not a conjunction, and thus cannot have a clause after it.

In the subordinate clause, use the subjunctive past perfect to indicate your unfulfilled wish about the event in an earlier time than the time expressed by the tense of the main verb.

Q: Correct the following sentence(s).

"Ten years ago, if my fans would not have gathered for me, I might have wept in front of the cameras," reminisces the singer now before an interviewer: The singer talks as if he saw angels in the crowd of fans ten years ago.

2.7.3 Subjunctive Present

Subjunctive present uses the base-form verbs in English; therefore, it has neither a tense nor a singular form. There are some verbs, nouns, and expressions that require a subjunctive present. Subjunctive present usually emphasizes importance, urgency, or indirect command.

2.7.3.1 Verbs and Nouns that Require a Subjunctive Present in the *that* Clause

> *Ex 1)*   *The pope <u>requested</u> (advise, ask, demand, desire, insist, order, prefer, propose, recommend, request, require, suggest, urge , etc.) <u>that</u> <u>every cardinal</u> in the world <u>come</u> to Vatican within a week.*

There are verbs, so-called *indirect-command verbs,* that require a subjunctive present in the following that clause. Notice that a base-form verb is used in the *that* clause even though the tense in the main clause is the past tense and the subject in the *that* clause is singular.

Nouns derived from these verbs also require a subjunctive in the following that clause.

> *Ex 2)*   *The <u>requirement</u> <u>that</u> <u>each criminal</u> <u>be</u> treated fairly is not followed properly in that nation.*

Again the base-form verb be is used regardless of the tense or the number of the subject.

☞ *Note*: When these verbs or nouns do not express an indirect command, you do not have to use a subjunctive present.

> *Ex 3)*   *He <u>suggested/insisted</u> that his roommates <u>were</u> liable for the damage, not he.*

> *Q: Correct the following sentence(s).*
>
> *The count asked that the countess presents herself before him as soon as she could.*

2.7.3.2 Adjectives that Require a Subjunctive Present in the *that* Clause

There are also adjectives, so-called *indirect-command adjectives,* that require a subjunctive present in the following *that* clause.

> *Ex 1)*   *It is <u>essential</u> that <u>everyone</u> <u>obey</u> this rule.*

Adjectives such as *essential, imperative, important, necessary, critical, mandatory, required,* and *vital* may require a verb word in the following *that* clause no matter what the tense or subject of the *that* clause is.

Q: Correct the following sentence(s).

The baron said that it was imperative that the baroness gives birth to a son to maintain his land.

2.8 Verbs that Require Only Infinitives or Only Gerunds as the Object

One of the most challenging grammatical rules of English pertains to the question of whether a transitive verb takes an infinitive or a gerund or both as its complement, and if both are allowed, whether they will give the same meaning.

2.8.1 Verbs that Require Infinitives, not Gerunds, in the Object

You can categorize these verbs like the following rather than simply memorize these verbs individually and independently. My categorization helped many students; nevertheless, if this doesn't help you much, just memorize them individually in your own way.

Ex 1)   I wish to keep in touch with you.

1) "Wish" verbs: *beg, wish, want, long, hope, desire, threaten, need* (remember *need* can take a verb word when it is used as a modal), etc.

2) "Plan" verbs: *plan, intend, expect, mean, prepare, promise, swear,* etc.

3) "Decide" verbs: *decide, agree, consent, hesitate, refuse,* etc.

4) Others: *afford, appear, arrange, claim, deserve, fail, learn, manage, offer, pretend, seem, struggle, tend, volunteer, wait,* etc.

2.8.2 Verbs that Require Infinitives as the Objective Complement

These verbs are often used in the BP5 pattern, in which they need an object (usually someone) and an objective complement (the action of that someone).

Ex 1)   I want you to listen to me very carefully.

The following verbs follow the same pattern when used in BP5.

1) "Ask" verbs: *ask, beg, convince, encourage, force, instruct, order, persuade, require, teach, tell, threaten, urge,* etc.

2) "Permit" *verbs: allow, permit, invite, forbid, grant,* etc.

3) Other verbs: *advise, cause, dare, expect, hire, need, remind, want, warn,* etc.

2.8.3 Verbs that Require Gerunds, not Infinitives, as the Object

Ex 1)   I had to <u>stop</u> <u>smoking</u> for my rehabilitation program.

Before I give these verbs, let me clarify one thing here. **This rule doesn't mean that these verbs can't be followed by infinitives; this simply means that infinitives cannot be used as the objects of these verbs.** See the following example.

Ex 2)   I had to <u>stop</u> <u>to smoke</u> because I had a sudden urge to smoke.

Here, the underlined infinitive *to smoke* is used as an adverb indicating the reason for stopping. Here, the verb *stop* is used as an intransitive verb, roughly meaning "stop walking." **This is why it is wise to avoid generalizing some grammatical rule unless you really know what is going on. You have to look at the context to determine the best expression out of all grammatically possible expressions.**

Anyway, here are the verbs of this kind that require gerunds as their objects.

1) "Stop" verbs: *complete, finish, quit, stop, keep, give up,* etc.

2) "Consider" verbs: *appreciate, consider, discuss, mind, miss, recall, recollect, understand,* etc.

3) "Suggest" verbs: *advise, mention, recommend, suggest,* etc.

4) Other verbs: *admit, anticipate, avoid, delay, deny, enjoy, postpone, resent, risk, tolerate,* etc.

☞ *Note*: One acronym that could be helpful in memorizing some of these gerund-requiring transitive verbs is **MEGAFACTS**, which is composed of the first letters of *mind, enjoy, give up, admit, finish, avoid, consider, tolerate,* and *suggest.*

5) Other verb phrases: *can't help, look forward to, object to, be used to, be accustomed to,* etc.

☞ *Note*: Special attention should be given to the fifth category. As discussed in section 2.3.3, the "*to*" used in these verb phrases or idioms are **prepositions**, not the "*to*" used in infinitives; that is why a gerund is used (because gerunds, not infinitives, are used as the object of the prepositions). **Again, distinguishing whether a "*to*" in a verb phrase is a preposition or part of an infinitive is very important.**

> *Q: Correct the following sentence(s).*
>
> *My scuba diving instructor told me that he intended spending more time with me because he could not tolerate to give a certificate to an unqualified diver.*

2.8.4 Verbs that Can Use Either Infinitives or Gerunds as the Object with Little or No Change in Meaning

Verbs such as *begin, start, continue, like, love, prefer, hate, can't stand, can't bear* can use either infinitives or gerunds with little or no change in meaning.

Ex 1)   *The Chicago Cubs fans can't stand to watch their team lose in Wrigley Field.*

≈ *The Chicago Cubs fans can't stand watching their team lose in Wrigley Field*

Ex 2)   *The skeptics prefer being doubtful to being credulous.*

≈ *The skeptics prefer to be doubtful than to be credulous.*

In the case of *prefer*, you have to use *to* when comparing gerunds and *than* when comparing infinitives. Idiomatically, however, using the preposition *to* with *prefer* is better.

☞ *Note*: There is a slight difference between using an infinitive and using a gerund even for these verbs. By using an infinitive, you basically tell the listener that you love or hate "your doing the action" whereas by using a gerund, you may imply that you love or hate "someone else's doing the action".

Ex 3)   *I hate to dance.* (you do not like to dance)
Ex 4)   *I hate dancing.* (you do not like dancing in general, even watching others dance)

2.8.5 Verbs that Can Use Either Infinitives or Gerunds with Some Change in Meaning

try, forget, remember

Ex 1)   The comedian *tried to make* the audience laugh.
(with an effort)
The comedian *tried making* the audience laugh.
(experimentally)

Ex 2)   Only two theologians in the seminary *remembered (forgot) to pray* before reading the Bible.
The monks *remember (forget) practicing* the lethal martial arts and *injuring* many people at the battle.

When used with infinitives as the object, *remember* and *forget* imply that the subject remembers or forgets **to perform some activity in the future**. On the other hand, when used with gerunds as the object, these verbs mean that the subject remembers or forgets **some activity that has already taken place; however**, nowadays, people more often use *having + p.p.* to indicate an activity that happend/had happened sometime before the action of remembering or forgetting occurs/occurred.

2.9 Causatives

Causatives are the verbs that cause someone or something to do something or to be changed. There are many verbs that cause or influence someone or something to do something, but the following five verbs are the most widely used causatives and are explained in the order of most forceful to least forceful. These verbs can be used as causatives as you could see in the BP5, the case of imperfect transitive verbs.

[Subject] + [Causative Verbs] + [Object(someone or something)] + [Objective Complement]

Depending on which causative is used and which voice (active or passive) between the object and the objective complement, the objective complement can take a base-form verb, an infinitive or a past participle. This is again one of the most peculiar eccentricities of English grammar which you may simply have to memorize.

Let's study them in detail.

2.9.1 Make

When *make* is used as a causative, the subject basically forces the object to do something (actively) or to receive the influence or change (passively).

> *Ex 1)*   *Steven Spielberg made the actor use more gestures.*
> (active relationship between the object(*the actor*) and the objective complement(*use*))

Here, the object (*the actor*) actively does the action of the objective complement (*use*). So in the active case, you use a base-form verb as the objective complement.

> *Ex 2)*   *Steven Spielberg made the scene (be) shortened.*
> (passive relationship between the object (*the scene*) and the objective complement (*(be) shortened)*))

Here the object (*the scene*) passively receives the action of the objective complement (*(be) shortened*).

☞ *Note*: However, this kind of usage of *make* is somewhat archaic. Nowadays, the use of *be* + *p.p.* for the objective complement of *make* in a passive case is rarely used. Actually, using *p.p* is also seldom used; you normally use a normal adjective like *short* instead of *shortened*.

2.9.2 Get

Get, when used as a causative, is very similar in meaning to *make* except the fact that it usually has less force and authority than *make*.

> *Ex 1)*   *The rioters got the politician to lead their cause.*
> (active relationship between the object (*the politician*) and the objective complement (*to lead*))

You use an infinitive as the active objective complement for the causative *get*.

> *Ex 2)*   *The rioters got the politician hanged.*
> (passive relationship between the object (*the politician*) and the objective complement (*hanged*))

You use a past participle as the passive objective complement for the causative *get*.

2.9.3 Have

Have, when used as a causative, is very similar in meaning to *get* except that it usually has less force and authority than *get*.

> *Ex 1)*   *My tutor will have me solve twice as many problems.*
> (active relationship between the object (*me*) and the objective complement (*solve*))

You use a base-form verb as the active objective complement for the causative *have*.

> *Ex 2)*   *The tutor will have the problems revised for me.*
> (passive relationship between the object (*the problems*) and the objective complement (*revised*))

You use a past participle as the passive objective complement for the causative *have*.

2.9.4 Let

Let, when used as a causative, expresses the action of giving someone permission to do something.

> *Ex 1)*   *The President let the director of CIA talk for an hour.*
> (active relationship b/w the object (*the director of CIA*) and the objective complement (*talk*))

You use a base-form verb as the objective complement for the causative *let*.

> *Ex 2)*   *The President let the congressman be assassinated.*

You use be-verb + p.p. as the passive objective complement. Like *make*, *let* is rarely used with the passive objective complement.

2.9.5 Help

Help, when used as a causative, expresses the action of aiding someone to do something.

> *Ex 1)*   *A duke from France will help the prince set up (or to set up) the international policy of our country .*
> (active relationship b/w the object (*the prince*) and the objective complement (*set up* or *to set up*))

You can use either a base-form verb or an infinitive as the active objective complement for the causative *help*.

> *Ex 2)* *A duke from France will help the prince be married (or to be married) to the princess of Spain.*
> (passive relationship b/w the object (*the prince*) and the objective complement (*be married* or *to be married*))

You use (*be-verb* + p.p.) or (to + *be-verb* + p.p.) as the passive objective complement for the causative *help*.

2.9.6 Summary Table of Causatives

Causatives	The form of the objective complement when the object does the action of the objective complement (Active)	The form of the objective complement when the object receives the action of the objective complement (Passive)
Make	The base form of a verb	(be) + p.p. (rarely used)
Get	infinitive	p.p.
Have	The base form of a verb	p.p.
Let	The base form of a verb	Be + p.p. (rarely used)
Help	The base form of a verb / infinitive	Be + p.p. / To be + p.p.

> *Q: Correct the following sentence(s).*
>
> *The soothsayer got me confess my background, but I made her to demonstrate her prescient power before I let my mouth spilling out secrets and get myself to be put in danger needlessly.*

2.10 Questions and Interrogatives

There are two kinds of questions: regular questions and special questions. Regular questions can be answered with "yes" or "no" whereas special questions cannot be answered that way.

2.10.1 Regular Questions

> *Ex 1)* *Did you fill up the tank with gas?*

Ex 2) <u>Have you been</u> to Korea?

Ex 3) <u>Is she sleeping</u> now? Was she exhausted?

Ex 4) <u>Can you come</u> to the volunteer project?

Regular questions start with auxiliary verbs. As in Ex 1, when no specific meaning needs to be added by an auxiliary verb, you simply use the *do/does/did* verbs. The word order for regular questions is

[Auxiliary verb] + [subject] + [verb or participles]

As you can see from the above examples, when you use modals or do-verbs, you have to use a base-form verb for the verb part after the subject (Ex 1 or Ex 4); when you use *have/has/had* to indicate the perfect tenses or when you use be-verbs to indicate the passive voice, you use past participles (Ex 2); and finally when you use be-verbs to indicate progressive tenses, you use present participles (Ex 3). As you can see, questions are a kind of **inversion**.

☞ **_Note_**: When asked a negative regular question, you answer the same as when you are asked a positive regular question. So, for example, if you answered "yes" to Ex 4, you will have to answer "yes" to the following question, too.

Ex 5) <u>Can't you come</u> to the volunteer project?
<u>Yes</u>. or <u>Yes, I can</u>.   <u>No</u>. or <u>No, I can't</u>.

2.10.2 Special Questions, Interrogatives, and Indirect Questions

Special questions start with interrogatives such as *who, what, which, when, where, how, why,* etc. **Depending on which role the interrogative takes, the word order of these special questions differ.**

Ex 1) <u>Who built</u> this building? Do you <u>know who built</u> this building?

<u>Whom did you</u> hire?   I <u>know whom you hired</u>.

Ex 2) <u>What caused</u> this mess? Did you <u>understand what caused</u> this mess?

<u>What did you</u> do? I don't <u>remember what you did</u>.

Ex 3) <u>Which was</u> his? Can you tell me <u>which was his</u>?

<u>Which did you</u> bring? Please, tell me <u>which you brought</u>.

Who, what, and *which*, when used in this way, are called *interrogative pronouns* and take the place of noun/pronoun as the subject or the object. In the first question of each example above, these interrogative pronouns are used as the subject of the sentence. Here, the interrogatives are themselves the subjects and does not require the help of auxiliary verbs. In the third question of each example, the interrogatives are used as the object, and you do see inversion.

☞ *Note*: When a special question is used as a part of a sentence such as the subject, the subjective complement, or the object, you call that sentence an **indirect question. In indirect questions**, as in the second and the fourth sentences of each example, **inversion is not there.**

Ex 4)   *When was his birthday? Do you know when his birthday was?*

When did you celebrate his birthday? Can you tell me when you celebrated his birthday?

Ex 5)   *Where were his friends? May I ask where his friends were?*

Where did the party take place? Will we find out where the party took place?

Ex 6)   *How was he at the party? Tell me how he was at the party.*

How did he invite that actress? Do you want me to confess to you about how he invited that actress?

Ex 7)   *Why was she late? I don't understand why she was late.*

Why did she do that? I don't see why she did that.

When, where, how, and *why*, used in this way, are called *interrogative adverbs* and take the place of adverbs and sometimes adjectives (as subjective complements). **Again, in indirect questions, inversion disappears.**

Ex 8)   *What/Which name are you using for your job? Can you tell me what/which name you are using for your job?*

What and *which*, when used in this way, are called *interrogative adjectives* since they modify the noun after them. **Again, when you use these clanses in indirect questions, the inversion has to disappear.**

> **Q: Correct the following sentence(s).**
>
> *Can somebody tell me when will he ask, "Can you allow me to explain why do I want to marry you?"*

2.11 Chapter Exam On Verbs

Find all grammar errors and correct them most efficiently. The following sentences may contain one, multiple, or no error(s).

1) Socrates born to a mason father and a midwife mother in 469 when the Sophists, the philosophers who enjoyed to argue with one another, was dominant.

2) Plato would not be able to establish Academia, the center of education in that era, if Socrates would not have influenced him, however, Plato created his own unique philosophy.

3) The ambition of the emperor had ended when he became seriously ill, so he requested that every child of his attended his presumably last birthday party.

4) The queen got her nephew take her throne, after hesitating for a while, he eventually accepted.

5) The admiral whose reputation is well-known in many countries say that he will construct 100 ships by the time the enemy invades our sea, yet the king does not believe what is he saying, fearing that he may fail accomplishing that project.

6) No sooner the car was fixed when my daughter drove it away.

7) Renowned for his brilliant expressions, people call the journalist "the word whiz," and his creative use of words made him to receive the prestigious journalist award.

8) When the imperial soldiers came back from the war, the Indian chief clearly remember them demolishing his land.

9) The physicist must be absorbed with his research when his fiancée came to see him: He did not see her for almost 3 years.

10) Unlike his predecessor, the new president was accustomed to speak in English while meeting with other CEOs; and also skilled in effective communication, his leadership was outstanding.

3 Noun

As discussed in the first chapter, noun is another essential part of speech in forming the essential parts of the sentence: the subject, the object, and the complement. A noun is classified as either countable or uncountable, but in many cases, depending on its use, a single noun can be at one time countable and at another time uncountable. There are some rules or patterns that determine which nouns are countable and which are uncountable; however, as is the case with most other grammatical rules, you cannot universally generalize these rules. Let's consider the peculiar aspects of nouns in English.

3.1 Countable Nouns

Ex 1)   We have <u>one million dollars</u>.

Countable nouns have both singular and plural forms. You can have plural numbers in front of countable nouns but not in front of uncountable nouns.

For the majority of countable nouns, you simply attach –s to form plural nouns; however, for many other nouns, you have to form plural nouns in the following ways:

- For nouns ending with *s, sh, z, x* or *ch* (if it sounds *tʃ*, not if it sounds *k*): attach -es.

  Ex 2)   match: matches, monarch: monarchs, bus: buses, brush: brushes, buzz: buzzes, box: boxes, etc.

☞ **Note**: Some nouns ending with –o need –es and some others need simply –s (usually the words from Spanish or Italian).

  Ex 3)   hero: heroes, potato: potatoes, veto: vetoes, alto: altos, casino: casinos, piano: pianos, studio: studios, etc.

- For nouns ending with [a consonant] + *y*: replace y with *ies* except in the case of proper nouns which take –s.

  Ex 4)   baby: babies, city: cities, reality: realities, Nancy: Nancys, etc.

☞ **Note**: Nouns with [a vowel] + *y* require only –s.

  Ex 5)   boy: boys, toy: toys, jay: jays, key: keys, etc.

- For nouns ending with *f* or *fe*: change *f* or *fe* to *ves*.

  Ex 6)   half: haves, leaf: leaves, life: lives, wife: wives, etc.

☞ **_Note_**: there are some nouns ending with *–f* that can take both *–s* or *–ves* even though using *–ves* is more formal.

  Ex 7)   hoof: hoofs/hooves, scarf: scarfs/scarves, staff: staffs/staves, wharf: wharfs/wharves, roof:roofs (rooves is not acceptable), *etc.*

- Numbers, letters, and symbols: attach apostrophe (') + s.

  Ex 8)   1980's (or 1980s), 9's, s's, #'s, %'s, etc.

Now, let's categorize the countable nouns.

- **Names or titles of persons or groups:**

  Ex 9)   girls, teachers, doctors, sons, families, countries, teams, organizations, etc.

- **Names of living things:**

  Ex 10)   cats, ants, horses, flowers, flies, locusts, etc.

- **Names of things with a definite, individual shape:**

  Ex 11)   chairs, desks, trucks, hotels, ships, books, bottles, jars, tanks, etc.

- **Units of measurement:**

  Ex 12)   meters, miles, yards, kilograms, degrees, hours, dollars, pieces, sheets, etc.

- **Some of the abstract concepts:**

  Ex 12)   jobs, rumors, sights, ideas, plans, laughs, facts, hints, etc.

Q: Correct the following sentence(s).

The studioes in that building are too expensive for me; furthermore, the wifes of my employees do not like their layouts.

3.2 Uncountable Nouns

Ex 1) <u>*Peace*</u> *is the greatest concern for most of the nations.*

Uncountable nouns don't have plural forms and are used only as singular nouns. Most of the time you don't use the definite article, *the*, in front of these nouns; however, as will be explained later, **this rule cannot be generalized, either (i.e., in some special situations, you may use *the* or even plural forms).**

Let's categorize the uncountable nouns:

- **Food, materials, or substances that can change their forms:**

  Ex 2) *water, meat, bread, milk, oil, gold, glass, wood, smoke, ice, carbon, steam, etc.*

- **Substances with many small parts:**

  Ex 3) *grain, rice, sand, salt, sugar, powder, etc.*

- **Groups of things with various sizes, shapes, and types:**

  Ex 4) *fruit, food, equipment, luggage, furniture, clothing, machinery, etc.*

- **Types of languages and fields of study:**

  Ex 5) *Korean, English, Spanish, anthropology, economics, biology, etymology, physics, etc.*

- **Games or Activities:**

  Ex 6) *basketball, Taekwondo, golf, poker, chess, Go-stop, swimming, hiking, billiards, dominoes, etc.*

- **Some of the abstract concepts, usually ending with –ness, -ance, -ence, -tion, -ity, -ery with a general meaning:**

  Ex 7) *peace, kindness, ignorance, confidence, education, beauty, grammar, vocabulary, etc.*

Q: Correct the following sentence(s).

The luggage my relatives brought through the customs contained a lot of furniture made of glasses.

3.3   Nouns with Countable and Uncountable meanings

Many nouns can be used as both countable and uncountable nouns; however, the meaning can change slightly depending on whether the noun is used as a countable or an uncountable noun. Two most common changes in meaning when a noun is used as countable or as uncountable are as follows:

- **Specific vs. General (or All):**

  Ex 1)   an agreement/agreements (an occasion or a document): agreement (abstract concept or all agreements)

  a business/businesses (a company): business (abstract concept or all business transactions)

  a language/languages (a specific language): language (abstract concept or all languages)

  a pain/pains (a specific occasion): pain (abstract concept or all pain), etc.

  Nouns such as *decision, education, history, honor, life, pleasure, prayer, silence, space, success, thought, time, war, work,* etc. belong to this category.

- **A separate thing/product vs. Material:**

  Ex 2)   a chicken/chickens (a living thing): chicken (meat or material for food), a cloth/cloths (a piece of cloth): cloth (material), a fire/fires (an event): fire (material), a glass/ glasses (a container): glass (material), a paper/papers (a document): paper (material), a stone/stones (a small piece of rock): stone (material), etc.

  Nouns such as *bone, iron, liquor,* etc. belong to this category.

  The above gives you a little sense about when and how uncountable nouns can be used as countable nouns and vice versa.

3.4 Uncountable Nouns that Are Usually Countable Nouns in Other Languages

There are many uncountable nouns in English that most learners tend to use as countable nouns. Let's take a look at some of these nouns:

advice, evidence, equipment, fun, furniture, homework, information, knowledge, leisure, luck, luggage, mail, money, music, news, poetry, rain, stuff, vocabulary, etc.

Even though some people are starting to use some of these as countable nouns, they are still widely considered as uncountable nouns and should not be used in the plural form.

> **Q: Correct the following sentence(s).**
> There are a lot of homeworks which require research into various kinds of equipments.

3.5 Uncountable Nouns in Singular or Plural Expressions

Depending on which uncountable nouns you want to singularize or pluralize, the units used to make them singular or plural differ. Let's look at some of the most widely used units.

- **A piece of / two pieces of:** *advice, bread, equipment, furniture, information, jewelry, luggage, mail, music, news, toast,* etc.

- **A sheet of / two sheets of:** *paper, board, cloth,* etc.

- **A slice of / two slices of:** *bread, cheese, ham,* etc.

  Other units are used for other specific nouns: <u>*a bar of*</u> *soap,* <u>*a bolt of*</u> *lighting,* <u>*a clap of*</u> *thunder,* <u>*a gust of*</u> *wind,* <u>*an ear*</u> *of corn,* <u>*a kernel/grain*</u> *of rice (wheat, corn, oat, etc.),* <u>*a loaf of*</u> *bread,* etc.

3.6 Special Nouns

There are some nouns that deserve some special attention because it is hard to see whether they are countable or uncountable.

3.6.1 Singular Nouns with –s

- **Games:** *billiards, checkers, dominoes, darts* (the game, not the pieces), etc.

- **Fields of study:** *economics, ethics, linguistics, mathematics, physics, politics, statistics, thermodynamics,* etc.

- **Diseases:** *diabetes, measles, mumps, rabies, rickets,* etc.

- Others: *customs* (the place where the bags are checked for illegal goods), *molasses, news, summons* (*summonses* for plural), etc.

☞ *Note*: Nouns that name single things that are made of two connected parts are considered plural.

Ex)   *eyeglasses, knickers, pants, pliers, scissors, sunglasses, tongs, trousers, tweezers,* etc.

3.6.2 Special Cases in which Plural Nouns Are Treated as Singular Nouns

There are special cases in which you have to treat certain plural nouns as singular. **In essence, when you refer to a single person or thing, you treat it as a singular noun even if it is a compound noun or in a plural form.**

Ex 1)   *The King and I is* a great movie. (the title of a work of art such as a book, movie, poem, painting, opera, statue, symphony, etc.)

Ex 2)   *The doctor and lawyer was really brilliant, but the general and the secretary were very stupid.* (the doctor and lawyer refers to a single person whereas *the general and the secretary* refer to two different people)

Ex 3)   *Five million dollars is needed for the project.* (phrases containing units of measurement such as *dollars, meters, miles, feet, pounds,* etc. because you consider them as a whole, not multiple amounts)

3.6.3 Nouns that Have the Same Form for Singular and Plural Cases

The following nouns use the same form for singular and plural cases:

- *means, series, species, barracks, gallows, etc.*

- *carp, deer, fish, salmon, sheep, trout, etc.*

- *Japanese, Chinese, Swiss, etc.* (but not for people like *Koreans* or *Americans*)

- *aircraft, spacecraft, etc.*

3.6.4 Irregular Nouns

- *Foot: feet, goose: geese, tooth: teeth, etc.*

- *Child: children, man: men, woman: women, person: persons or people, etc.*

- *Louse: lice, mouse: mice, etc.*

3.6.5 Nouns that Have Special Plural Forms

There are some other nouns, usually scientific terms from Latin and Greek, that have different plural forms.

- *Analysis: analyses, axis: axes, basis: bases, crisis: crises, hypothesis: hypotheses, etc.*

- *Alumnus: alumni, focus: foci, fungus: fungi, nucleus: nuclei, syllabus: syllabi, stimulus: stimuli, etc.*

- *Criterion: criteria, phenomenon: phenomena, etc.*

- *Alga: algae, nebula: nebulae, pupa: pupae, vertebra: vertebrae, etc.*

- *Appendix: appendices, index: indices (appendixes, indexes are still accepted by some), etc.*

- *Datum: data, honorarium: honoraria, medium: media(mediums, if refering to people through whom the dead speak), stratum: strata, etc.*

3.6.6 Collective Nouns

Ex 1) *The jury was determined to put the criminal into a prison cell.*

In American English, collective nouns such as *audience, class, club, community, crowd, entourage, jury, swarm,* etc. are customarily considered singular unless you attach –s to make them groups of people, animals, etc. Nevertheless, when you want to refer to the individual members of the group, they can be treated as plural nouns.

Ex 2) *My family are all healthy because of good genetics.*
(individual members are all healthy)

There are also some collective nouns that are usually considered plural: *cattle, people, police,* etc., but *police* are normally not modified by adjectives such as several.

Ex 3) *The police/the cattle/the people are here. Several people / several cattle (*but not *several police) were injured.*

Note: *people* can also have –s attached to it; however, *peoples* means different tribes or nationalities rather than persons.

Ex 4) *The peoples of ancient Asia were mostly belligerent.*

Q: Correct the following sentence(s).
The evening news were reporting that diabetes are becoming a serious social problem for the womans according to the recent analysises conducted by one of my alumnuses.

3.7 Nominal Phrases and Clauses

3.7.1 Nominal Infinitive Phrases and Gerund Phrases

Ex 1) *To learn English and math as much as possible is our family's goal.* (subject)

Ex 2) *The most important thing is to learn English and math as much as possible.* (subjective complement)

Ex 3) I intend *to learn English and math as much as possible.*
(object of a verb)

Ex 4) I encouraged my friend to *learn English and math as much as possible.* (objective complement)

Nominal infinitive phrases can be used in the place of the subject, the subjective complement, the object, and the objective complement. Nominal gerund phrases can be used in the same way; you can simply replace the underlined words in Ex 1 and Ex 2 with *learning English and math as much as possible.*

However, in the place of the object of a preposition, you have to use a gerund phrase rather than an infinitive phrase.

Ex 5) I could not *insist* *on* *staying* longer in her house.

☞ **Note**: For Ex 3, whether to use an infinitive phrase or a gerund phrase depends on the verb. In Ex 3, an infinitive phrase is used because the verb *intend* takes only an infinitive as the object. Refer to section 2.8, Verbs that Require Only Infinitives or Only Gerunds as the Object.

3.7.2 Nominal Clauses

There are many ways for a clause to be used as a noun and come into the place of the subject, the subjective complement, or the object.

3.7.2.1 Nominal *That* Clause

Ex 1) *That we are brothers and sisters* is an undeniable fact.
(as a subject)

Ex 2) The truth is *that we are of the same bloodline.* (as a subjective complement)

Ex 3) Do you really believe *that we have the same parents?*
(as an object)

Ex 4) I find it unbelievable *that you are of the same kind.* (with an empty pronoun *it* which in this case refer to *that you are of the same kind*: refer to It – the Empty Subject or Object in section 3.8)

A conjunction *that* is interpreted here as *the fact/the idea that* ; thus, *that* clauses used in this way are nominal and take the place of the subject, the subjective complement, or the object.

3.7.2.2 Nominal Interrogative Clause

Ex 1)   <u>When (where, why, how) he buried her</u> *is a mystery.*
(as a subject)

Ex 2)   *The mystery is* <u>when (where, why, how) he buried her.</u>
(as a subjective complement)

Ex 3)   *Do you know* <u>when (where, why, how) he buried her?</u>
(as an object)

Interrogatives *when, where, why* and *how* can be interpreted as *the time when, the place where, the reason that* and *the way how*, respectively. In this case, these clauses are used as nouns and can be used as the subject, the subjective complement, or the object.

☞ *Note*: You cannot use inversion for these nominal interrogative clauses because these are used as a part of the sentence as in an indirect question.

Ex 4)   <u>Who (Which, What) buried her</u> *is a mystery.*

Interrogatives *who, which,* and *what* can be interpreted as *the person(s) who, the thing(s) which,* and *the thing(s) that*, respectively. In that case, these clauses are used as nouns and can be used as a subject, a subjective complement, or an object. Again, notice that there is no inversion in these nominal interrogative clauses.

☞ *Note*: The above statement should not be interpreted to mean that these interrogatives are always used nominally. This usage is just one of many usages of interrogatives. Refer to Special Questions, Interrogatives, and Indirect Questions (Section 2.10.2)

Ex 5)   <u>What (Which, Whose) money was stolen</u> *is the crucial question.* (as a subject)

What, which, and *whose* used in this way is called interrogative adjectives because they modify the noun right after it.

Ex 6)   *I told my heir* <u>whom he can trust</u> *and* <u>who committed that crime.</u> (used as objective complements)

> Ex 7)   I will give my authority <u>to whoever is the wisest</u> and <u>to whomever the majority of people will select.</u>

Interrogative adjectives can also lead a nominal clause as the example above shows and can take the place of the subject, the subjective complement, the object, and the object of the preposition.

3.7.2.3 Nominal *If/Whether* Clause

> Ex 1)   The question is <u>if she dumped you.</u> The question is <u>whether she dumped you (or not).</u> (as a subjective complement)

> Ex 2)   Does he know <u>if she dumped you?</u> Does he know <u>whether she dumped you (or not)?</u> (as an object)

> Ex 3)   <u>Whether she dumped you or not</u> is the main issue. (as a subject)

If and *whether* can both be used as a subjective complement or an object, but usually only a *whether* clause, not an *if* clause, is used as a subject.

Q: Correct the following sentence(s).

My coach is ~~asking~~ all of us to participate in ~~to play for~~ the fundraising, but ~~if~~ he will join the game is yet unknown.

whether

3.8   Chapter Exam on Nouns

Find all grammar errors and correct them most efficiently. The following
sentences may contain one, multiple, or no error(s).

1) The teacher is nicknamed "the walking dictionary," because he
has memorized entire dictionary that contains 60,000 words

2) "The boisterous crowd of millions of indignant people are
marching toward the state capitol, but five miles of walking are
not easy for most of them," reported the veteran reporter about
one of the emerging phenomenons.

3) Billiards are one of the best sports that gentlemen can enjoy
because simple physics are all it requires.

4) The friend and patron were the one I chose as the godfather for
my son, for the criterions I applied are integrity and
trustworthiness.

5) When I heard those five loud thunders, I began to shudder
involuntarily because of the nightmarish poetries I had read
when the only pair of eyeglasses I had were broken.

4 Pronoun

Pronouns are just like nouns in their roles; they are used in the place of the subject, the subjective complement, the object, the objective complement, or the object of prepositions. Possessive pronouns (also called pronominal adjectives: *my, your, our, his, her, their,* etc) are used as adjectives. There are definite pronouns and indefinite pronouns. Definite pronouns are used in the place of nouns to avoid repetition of the same nouns (*he, she, it, they,* etc.). The noun that a definite pronoun refers to is called the "**antecedent** of the pronoun." There are three cases of pronouns: subjective (sometimes called nominative), objective, and possessive. There are also reflexive pronouns, relative pronouns, and reciprocal pronouns. Let's study what they are and how they are used.

4.1 Subjective Pronouns

> *Ex 1)*   *My sister and he will do the chores.*

You have to use subjective pronouns in the subject's place. This rule also applies to compound subjects. Subjective pronouns are *I, you, he/she, it, we, you,* and *they.*

> *Ex 2)*   *It is I whom she is in love with.*

> *Ex 3)*   *The frog became he.*

You have to use subjective pronouns also in the subjective complement's place that come after BP2 verbs (the linking verbs) such as be-verbs, state-of-being verbs, and BP2 sensory verbs. In casual speech, however, people often use an objective case in the subjective complement's place.

☞ *Note*: **Nevertheless, in formal writing, avoid using an objective pronoun in the subjective complement's place.**

> *Q: Correct the following sentence(s).*
> The persons who have to take the ultimate responsibility is my wife and me because both she and me know that we promised satisfactory results.

4.2 Objective Pronouns

Ex 1) The director of marketing <u>replaced</u> him <u>with</u> her.

You have to use objective pronouns in the object's place after transitive verbs. Objective pronouns are *me, you, him/her, it, us, you,* and *them*.

Also, you have to use objective pronouns after prepositions such as *above, among, below, between, by, for, from, of, on, to, with,* etc. The nouns/pronouns that come after the prepositions are called the objects of the prepositions. Refer to chapter 7 on prepositions.

Ex 2) <u>Between</u> the committee members and <u>me</u>, nothing is hidden.

Q: Correct the following sentence(s).

The subtle and fragile relationship <u>between</u> the president, a very
conservative man, and I, a very liberal woman, reminds me of that
between my dad's boss and he.

4.3 Possessive Pronouns

Ex 1) <u>Their</u> <u>contribution</u> to the project was considerable.

Ex 2) <u>Her</u> <u>leg</u> was broken when she fell from the second floor.

There are two kinds of possessive pronouns. The first kind is virtually always used as adjectives because these pronouns modify the noun that follows; they are more precisely called **pronominal adjectives.** These adjectives have the same role as nouns + apostrophe, indicating someone's or something's ownership. These possessive pronouns are *my, your, his, her, its, our, your,* and *their*. As you can see from Ex 2, you often use possessive pronouns before a body part.

Ex 3) The soldiers insisted on <u>his</u> <u>staying</u> with them.

Ex 4) Billions of people will benefit from <u>his</u> <u>suffering</u> the brutal death.

Because gerunds act as nouns, to modify a gerund or to indicate its subject (in the cases it cannot be omitted because the meaning changes if not given), you use the possessive case. **Using objective pronouns instead of possessive pronouns in front of GERUNDS is another very commonly-made mistake, and you must avoid it in formal writing.** Refer to section 2.4.2.

The second kind of possessive pronouns (*mine, yours, his, hers, its, ours, yours,* and *theirs*) are used as nouns rather than adjectives. These pronouns substitute for a noun or noun phrase that refers to the object possessed.

Ex 5)   All of the purple marbles are *mine.*

Ex 6)   The archbishop is a friend of *mine.*

A friend of *mine* in Ex 6 is an often-used expression meaning *one* of *my friends* and is different from the expression, *my friend.* It follows the structure, [*A/an*] + [noun such as *friend, son, daughter, colleague, teacher,* etc.] + [*of*] + [possessive pronoun such as *mine, yours, his/hers, ours, theirs,* etc.].

Q: Correct the following sentence(s).
My pastor was greatly worried about me missing the baptism ceremony because last year a daughter of him missed it.

4.4 Noun-Pronoun Agreement

Error 1) When the <u>rascals</u> tried to tease the substitute teacher who looked inexperienced, she warned <u>him</u> to focus on the class work.

Whenever a pronoun refers to a noun in the sentence or even the previous sentences, it has to agree with the noun in number and gender; thus, the pronoun *him* that refers to *rascals* must be corrected to *them.*

Error 2) When <u>one</u> doesn't have a legitimate visa to the U.S.A., <u>you</u> will be required to leave the country.

Because an indefinite pronoun *one* was used in the first clause, the subject of the main clause *you* should also be *one.*

4.5 Reflexive Pronouns

Ex 1)   It is very difficult for <u>a really talented person</u> to humble <u>himself</u> or <u>herself</u>.

Ex 2)   <u>I</u> was very proud of <u>myself</u> for the landslide victory.

You use reflexive pronouns when the object of a verb or a preposition is the same as the subject. Reflexive pronouns are formed by attaching *self* for singular pronouns and *selves* for plural pronouns to the objective case or the possessive case: *myself, yourself, himself, herself, itself, ourselves, yourselves,* and *themselves.*

Ex 3) The Bible says that <u>God Himself</u> had to come to the earth and pay for the price of the sins of men.

A reflexive pronoun can also be used to emphasize the noun/pronoun in front of it.

Ex 4) Who can study English <u>by himself/herself?</u>

[by] + [reflexive pronoun] means *alone.*

> **Q: Correct the following sentence(s).**
> "You have to love ~~you~~ yourself and be proud of ~~you~~ yourself," preached the cult leader who built the entire congregation by himself

4.6 Reciprocal Pronouns (Each Other, One Another)

Ex 1) <u>My parents</u> love <u>each other</u> very much; <u>they</u> look <u>at each other</u> every available moment.

Ex 2) <u>My children</u> love <u>one another.</u>

Reciprocal pronoun phrases *each other* or *one another* can be used as the object or as the object of a preposition when you want to express a reciprocal act of the plural subject. Formally, *each other* is for two people or things whereas *one another* is for three or more people or things, even though many writers use *each other* for more than two people or things.

4.7 Consecutive Order

4.7.1 One, Another, The Other

> *Ex 1)* *The king had three sons; <u>one</u> is very smart, <u>another</u> is very strong, and <u>the other</u> is very handsome.*

> *Ex 2)* *<u>One</u> <u>class</u> is Economics, <u>another</u> <u>class</u> is Psychology, and <u>the other</u> <u>class</u> is Linear Algebra.*

One, another, and *the other* are used for indicating consecutive order for three persons/things. Ex 1 shows the case in which these are used as pronouns whereas Ex 2 shows the case in which these are used as adjectives modifying the singular countable nouns after them. Notice that only singular countable nouns can be used after *one* and *another*. Refer to other ways to indicate consecutive order using ordinal numbers in Section 5.4.

4.7.2 Some, Others, The Others (or The Rest)

> *Ex 1)* *There are many talented students in our school; <u>some</u> are musical, <u>others</u> are athletic, and <u>the others</u> (or <u>the rest</u>) are artistic.*

> *Ex 2)* *<u>Some</u> <u>churches</u> are Presbyterian, <u>other</u> <u>churches</u> are Methodist, and <u>the other</u> (or <u>the rest of the</u>) <u>churches</u> are Baptist.*

Some, others, and *the others* are used to indicate a consecutive order for many persons/things (obviously at least more than three), and using them covers the entire group (i.e., every item in the group belongs to one of the three subgroups). Ex 1 shows the case in which these are used as pronouns whereas Ex 2 shows the case in which these are used as adjectives modifying the plural nouns after them. *Others* becomes *other* and *the other* (or *the rest*) becomes *the other* (or *the rest of the*) when used as an adjective. Notice that only plural countable nouns can be used after these in this structure.

Q: Correct the following sentence(s).   one another

My twelve grandsons are in good terms with each other; the others
Interestingly, some are pastors, another are monks, and the other are
                                        others are
rabbis.

4.8   It – the Empty Subject or Object

Ex 1)   It is disturbing to see my friend fight.

≈To see my friend fight is disturbing.

Ex 2)   It looks as if the king will visit our town.

Here, *it* is used as an empty subject and has no specific meaning. *It*, when used in this way, is sometimes called an expletive (9.2). An empty subject *it* is often used when the real subject is long or when you want to emphasize the adjective (in Ex 1, *disturbing*).

Ex 3)   The judge made it clear that there will be no further hearing.

≈That there will be no further hearing was made clear by the judge.

Here, *it* is used as an empty object and has no meaning. An empty object *it* is often used when the real object is a *that* clause in BP5 (the incomplete transitive verb).

4.9   Indefinite Pronouns

4.9.1 Singular Indefinite Pronouns

Ex 1)   Each of the students has to pay his or her tuition for the trimester.

[*each, one, either, neither, every one,* etc.] + [of] + [the] + [plural countable noun] + [singular verb]

Ex 2)   Everyone knows that proverb.

[*everyone, anyone, someone, no one, somebody, everybody, anybody, each, one, either, neither, this, that,* etc.] + [singular verb]

Ex 3)   Neither student meets the criteria.

[*each, one, either, neither, every, another, this, that,* etc.] + [singular noun]

In this case, these words are used as adjectives.
(Refer to 5.3 Ways to Express Quantity)

Q: *Correct the following sentence(s).*
Every students claimed that neither of teachers were eligible to teach the advanced classes; everybody who knows them refutes that claim.

[handwritten annotations: *student*, *subject*, *the*, *was*, *knew*, *Even*]

4.9.2 Plural Indefinite Pronouns

Ex 1) *These are too costly to buy.*

[*these, those,* etc.] + [plural verb]

Ex 2) *Those scoundrels want to kidnap the millionaire.*

[*these, those,* etc.] + [plural nouns] + [plural verb]

In this case, these words are used as adjectives.

4.9.3 Indefinite Pronouns Whose Numbers Depend on the Following Noun

Ex 1) *All of the pupils are invited*

[*all, any, some, most, none, more,* etc.] + [of] + [the] +
[plural countable noun] + [plural verb]

Ex 2) *All of the money we had is gone.*

[*all, any, some, most, none, more,* etc.] + [of] + [the] +
[uncountable noun] + [singular verb]

These pronouns can be used as adjectives, too.
(Refer to 5.3 Ways to Express Quantity)

Q: *Correct the following sentence(s).*
It has been confirmed that none of the novels written by that author was recommendable and that most of the information given there were misleading.

[handwritten annotations: *subject*, *This*, *were*, *was*]

4.10 Relative Pronouns

Grammatical rules for the usage of relative pronouns may look complicated for foreigners. Let's study different kinds of relative pronouns and their usages. Relative pronouns lead relative clauses and modify the noun/pronoun in front of them; thus, relative pronoun clauses are, in their role, **adjectival clauses.**

4.10.1 Relative Pronouns that Refer to Persons

- **Subjective Relative Pronoun: Who**

   Ex 1)   *That girl is the violinist who ruined the symphony in the concert.*

   ≈That girl is the violinist. The violinist ruined the symphony in the concert.

The subjective relative pronoun *who* connects two clauses by substituting for the subject of the following clause whose subject refers to the antecedent (in this case, *the violinist*).

   Ex 2)   *That girl is the violinist who the real heroine of the whole concert is.*

   ≈That girl is the violinist. The real heroine of the whole concert is the violinist.

Who is also used to replace the subjective complement. Avoid using whom in this case.

☞ *Note*: This is so even when you have a short inserted phrase such as *I believe, I think*, etc.

   Ex 3)   *That girl is the violinist who (I believe) is the real heroin of the whole concert.*

   ≈That girl is the violinist. I believe the violinist is the real heroin of the whole concert.

Notice that *who* in the example above is not the object of the verb *believe*.

- **Objective Relative Pronoun: Whom**

> *Ex 4)* *That girl is <u>the violinist</u> <u>whom</u> everybody gave a big hand.*
>
> *≈That girl is <u>the violinist</u>. Everybody gave <u>her</u> a big hand.*

The objective relative pronoun *whom* connects two clauses by substituting the object of the following clause where its object (in this case, *her*) is the same as the antecedent (again, *the violinist*).

> *Ex 5)* *That girl is <u>the violinist from</u> <u>whom</u> the conductor received money.*
>
> *≈That girl is <u>the violinist</u>. The conductor received money <u>from her</u>.*

Here, the object relative pronoun *whom* refers to the object of the preposition *from*. You may put *from* at the end of the sentence, but by putting it in front of *whom*, you allow the listeners to expect how that antecedent will be used in the following clause, so this way is often preferred.

☞ *Note*: You have to be able to distinguish prepositions in prepositional phrases from **particles** which are components of phrasal verbs (particles will be covered in the chapter on preposition). With particles, you cannot use the structure in Ex 5 (i.e. you cannot put the particle in front of the relative pronoun). Refer to Preposition vs Particle (7.3).

> *Ex 6)* *I know many geniuses, <u>one</u> (or each, either, neither, or any other singular nouns) of whom is my own son.*
>
> *≈I know many <u>geniuses</u>. <u>One</u> (or each, either, neither, or any other singular nouns) of <u>them</u> <u>is</u> my own son.*

☞ *Note*: When the relative pronoun is used as the subject in the relative pronoun clause, *who* instead of *whom* should be used even after a preposition.

> *Ex 7)* *I will listen <u>to whom</u> (whomever) my people select.* (because *whom* is used as the object of *select* in the following clause)
>
> *Ex 8)* *I will listen <u>to who</u> (whoever) has my people's trust.* (because *who* is used as the subject of the following clause)

- **Possessive Relative Pronoun: Whose**

> *Ex 10)* *That girl is* *the violinist* *whose father is the conductor.*
>
> ≈*That girl is* *the violinist. Her father is the conductor.*

The possessive relative pronoun *whose* connects two clauses by substituting for the possessive noun/pronoun of the following clause in which the possessive noun/pronoun (in this case, the possessive case pronoun *her*) is the same as the antecedent (again, *the violinist*).

Q: Correct the following sentence(s).

There arose many pioneers, *each of who were* about to become a Nobel laureate; some of them were also political activists *whom* ideas were also iconoclastic and from *who* numerous new movements would ensue.

[handwritten: whom, was, whose, winner, subject, whom]

[handwritten: Iconoclastic → breaking cherished traditions]

4.10.2 Relative Pronouns that Refer to Things

[handwritten: → whichjin which; where]

- **Which**

> *Ex 1)* *Chris broke* *the toy which was his brother's favorite.*
>
> ≈*Chris broke* *the toy. The toy was his brother's favorite.*

> *Ex 2)* *Chris broke* *the toy, which his father gave him.*
>
> ≈*Chris broke* *the toy. His father gave him* *the toy.*

The relative pronoun *which* can be used as a subject or an object as the examples above show. When *which* refers to a possessive case pronoun or noun, you use *of which* in the following way.

> *Ex 3)* *Chris broke* *the toy, the color of which is turquoise.*
>
> ≈*Chris broke* *the toy, whose color is turquoise.*
>
> ≈*Chris broke* *the toy. The toy's color is turquoise.*

☞ **Note**: *Whose* could also be used instead of *of which* even for nonhuman things in a possessive case.

☞ **Note**: *That* can replace *which* in subjective or objective cases for nonhuman things; however, *that* is used only for restrictive case whereas *which* could be used for both restrictive and nonrestrictive cases (see 4.10.4).

4.10.3 Other Relative Pronouns

When/where/why/how can be used as relative pronouns and take a time/place/reason/way as their antecedents, respectively.

☞ **_Note_**: In formal writing, the relative pronoun *when* must have a specific time as its antecedent (for example, 1999 *when ~, the 20th century when ~*, etc.) and the relative pronoun where must have a specific place as its antecedent (for example, *Seoul where ~, a park where*, etc.). Otherwise, you have to use [adequate preposition such as *in*] + [*which*].

Error 1) *I encountered really enervating situations* <u>*when/where*</u> *I lost all hope.*

Corr 1) *I encountered really enervating situations* <u>*in which*</u> *I lost all hope.*

Error 2) *The* <u>*circumstances*</u> <u>*when*</u> *the director struggled resulted in an ugly* <u>*crisis*</u> <u>*where*</u> *everyone had to leave the company.*

Corr 2) *The* <u>*circumstances*</u> <u>*with which*</u> *the director struggled resulted in an ugly* <u>*crisis*</u> <u>*in which*</u> *everyone had to leave the company.*

Q: Correct the following sentence.

King Sejong is Korea's greatest inventor ~~whom~~ who *, in harsh* <u>*circumstances*</u> *when many people opposed his proposition,* <u>*created*</u> *Hangul, the current Korean language which alphabet is amazingly simple and scientific.*

① The alphabet which ...
② whose alphabet

4.10.4 Restrictive Vs Nonrestrictive Relative Pronouns

restrictive

Ex 1)   *The architect who designs skyscrapers will be demanded more by the present market.* (restrictive)

≈*Any architect who designs skyscrapers will be demanded more by the present market.*

nonrestrictive

Ex 2)   *The architect, who designs skyscrapers, will be demanded more by the present market.* (nonrestrictive)

≈*The architect, who can be further described as one who designs skyscrapers, will be demanded more by the present market.*

The first example is using a restrictive relative pronoun *who* whereas the second example is using a nonrestrictive relative pronoun *who*. For a nonrestrictive case, you put commas around the relative clause, and for a restrictive case, you do not. Notice the difference in meanings between the two cases. In a nonrestrictive case, you just give additional information about the antecedent *architect* whom you already know even without that additional information. However, in a restrictive case, you give essential information about the antecedent, thereby restricting its referent (i.e., any skyscraper-designing architect will be demanded).

☞ *Note*: The relative pronoun *that* is used only for restrictive cases whereas *which* could be used for both restrictive and nonrestrictive cases even though some grammarians prefer *that* for restrictive cases.

☞ *Note*: **You can omit objective relative pronouns in restrictive cases** both for human and nonhuman antecedents, but **not in nonrestrictive cases**. You should be able to tell that the second clause is a relative pronoun clause even though you do not see an objective relative pronoun; in other words, you should not regard this structure as a run-on-sentence.

Ex 3)   *This is the city () he likes most.*

Ex 4)   *Did you see the movie () my best friend was in?*

4.11 Chapter Exam on Pronouns

Find all grammar errors and correct them most efficiently. The following sentences may contain one, multiple, or no error(s).

1) The four defendants were us, and the justice ordered every one of we defendants not to talk to each other during the hearing.

2) Because only the Constitution can mediate between the unbridled authoritarian government and we, our senators, after listening to the director, objected to him speaking against the U.S. Constitution and said that he should be ashamed of him for doing them.

3) The athlete is the one that received the gold medal and made a sensation where our countrymen became obsessed with them following in his footsteps.

4) At the end of the day, the computer, that was developed most recently, will dominate their market.

5) God will show his mercy to whomever will obey His commandments, and His servants in that church, whom I believe has great faith, will be abundantly rewarded.

5   Adjective

Adjectives modify and describe nouns. One convenient fact about adjectives is that unlike verbs or nouns, they, except in the case with the indefinite article (*a/an*), do not change their forms. There are various kinds of adjectives, and let us study the important and confusing kinds in this chapter.

5.1   Determiner

> *Ex 1)*   <u>*Each*</u> *person does his job without* <u>*any*</u> *help.*

> *Ex 2)*   <u>*All*</u> *members have to peruse* <u>*these*</u> *manuscripts.*

Special non-descriptive adjectives used in front of nouns to determine which specific entity/entities those nouns represent are called **determiners**. Some of the examples of determiners are *a/an, the, this, that, each, every, any, some, no, such, both, few, a few, little, a little, many, much, all,* etc. (most of these determiners can also be used as indefinite pronouns as shown in section 4.9). The kinds of nouns (singular/plural countable nouns or uncountable nouns) that these determiners can modify differ. Those rules will be covered in detail in section 5.3. The most important and common are the articles, *a/an/the,* covered in the next section.

5.2   Article

One of the most troublesome sets of grammatical rules for foreigners, especially Koreans, is the rules for the article. An **article** is either the indefinite article *a/an* or the definite article *the*. Basically, you have to put *a/an/the* (or some of the other possible determiners) in front of **any singular countable noun,** except for some idiomatic cases. Let's study when and how they are used.

5.2.1 A/An

> *Ex 1)*   *There is* <u>*a*</u> *beautiful single* <u>*woman.*</u>

> *Ex 2)*   *There is* <u>*an*</u> *ugly single* <u>*woman.*</u>

A/an is called the indefinite article because they indicate no particular person(s) or thing(s). The indefinite article *a/an* is one of the determiners. *A/an* means one and is used before singular countable nouns only. *A* is used before words that begin with a consonant pronunciation whereas *an* is used before words that begin with a vowel pronunciation.

☞ *Note*: Be careful of the nouns that start with a consonant letter that is not pronounced.

> *Ex 3)*   *An hour has passed and an heir must be announced now.*

Words such as *hour, heir, honor,* etc., for example, starts with *h* but the first pronunciation is a vowel rather than a consonant.

☞ *Note*: Also be careful of the nouns that start with a vowel letter that is pronounced like a consonant.

> *Ex 4)*   *A usual offer is a use of the park for the whole year.*

Words such as *unique, university, universe, use, usual*, etc., start with a vowel alphabet *u* but sounds like *y*, a consonant.

5.2.2 Word Order for Phrases Starting with *So, As, How, Too* and *Such, Quite, What*

> *Ex 1)*   It is *so beautiful a day* for a picnic. It is *as great a day* as last
> Sunday. *How wonderful a day* (it/this is)! It is indeed *too nice*
> *a day* to stay at home.

For *so, as, how*, and *too*, the word order is

[*so/as/how/too*] + [adjective] + {[*a/an*] + [singular noun]}

I used examples that show typical usage of *as* (used for comparison) and *too* (used with an infinitive indicating the impossibility of the action). For these, the phrase in the {} is optional (i.e., you may or may not add that structure)

> *Ex 2)*   It is *such a beautiful day* for a picnic. It is *quite a nice day* for
> fishing. *What an amazing day* (it/this is)!

For *such, quite*, and *what*, the word order is

[*such/quite/what*] + [*a/an*] + {[adjective]} + [singular noun]

For these, you can omit the adjective part.

☞ *Note*: *So* cannot be used for **plural nouns** and **uncountable nouns**. Thus, avoid using *so* for them.

> *Error 1) These are so delicious dishes. It is so great advice that I cannot ignore it.*

> *Error 2) They are so smart boys as your children. My boss reported so great news as the news you reported yesterday.*

> *Corr 1) These are such delicious dishes. It is such great advice that I cannot ignore it.*

> *Corr 2) They are as smart boys as your children. My boss reported as great news as the news you reported yesterday.*

Q: Correct the following sentence(s).

When you produce such amazing an artifact, the queen will award an honor to you in this quite productive a season because it is too an adorable piece to ignore.

5.2.3 *The*

> *Ex 1)   Did you finish the project that the CEO gave you a month ago?*

The definite article *the* is used before a noun when the speaker and the listener know which specific person(s)/thing(s) is/are referred to. In other words, they know which specific person(s)/thing(s) is/are being mentioned. *The* can be used for singular and plural countable nouns as well as for uncountable nouns.

5.2.3.1 *The* for Generic Countable Nouns

A generic noun means the noun that indicates the whole group of things in a category. Usually, *a/an* or plural nouns are used to establish a generic meaning for countable nouns; however, there are nouns that use *the* instead for the generic meaning.

- Musical instruments: the guitar, the piano, the cello, the trumpet, the keyboard, the bass, the drum, etc.

- Inventions: the computer, the monitor, the elevator, the television, the radio, etc.

- Nationality that ends with *s, ch, sh, z*: *the French, the Irish, the Finnish,* etc. (in this case we are talking about the people of those nationalities; thus, you have to use plural verbs when these appear as subjects)

☞ **Note**: You can always use *a/an* or plural nouns for these when we are not talking about the group as a whole (i.e. generic meaning) but rather as individual entities.

> *Ex 1) There are five <u>computers</u> in the room that also has five <u>pianos</u>.*

5.2.3.2 The for Proper Nouns

There are proper nouns that use *the* in front of them.

- **Mountains, oceans, seas, rivers, islands, peninsulas, canals, deserts, etc.:** mountains (*the Himalayas, the Andes, the Rocky, the Alps*), oceans (*the Pacific, the Atlantic, the Indian*), seas (*the Caribbean Sea, the Gulf of Mexico, the Red Sea*), rivers (*the Nile, the Yangtze, the Han, the Mississippi*), islands (*the Cayman Islands, the Philippines, the British Isles*), *the Korean Peninsula, the Suez Canal, the Sahara Desert,* etc.

☞ **Note**: Place names that are plural start with *the*.

> *Ex 1) the Great Lakes, the Andes Mountains, the British Isles, etc.*

☞ **Note**: The names of a single mountain (not mountain ranges) and of a single island usually do not have *the*.

> *Ex 2) Manhattan Island, Mount Everest, Lake Michigan, etc.*

☞ **Note**: Place names that have qualifying phrases starting with *of* usually have *the*.

> *Ex 3) the Cape of Good Hope, the Isle of Man, the Gulf of Mexico, etc.*

- **United entities:** *the United Nations, the United States of America, the United Kingdom, the Netherlands,* etc.

- **Unique architectures:** *the White House, the Capitol, the Lincoln Memorial, the Museum of Science and Industry,* etc.

- **Ships, space shuttles, etc.:** *the May Flower, the Queen Elizabeth II, the Titanic, the Confederate, the Apollo XIII, the Concord, etc.*

- **Newspapers, magazines, etc.:** *the New York Times, the Washington Post, the Chicago Tribune, the Times, the U.S. News, etc.*

5.2.3.3 *The* for Uncountable Nouns (Usually Followed by Qualifying Phrases)

It has been mentioned that uncountable nouns in general cannot have *the* in front of them; however, when they refer to a specific thing or concept, *the* normally does modify the nouns.

Ex 1) *The water of the Nile River is nowadays a little bit dirty.*

Here *the* modifies *water*, which is an uncountable noun, because you have *of the Nile River* modifying, qualifying, and specifying it, thereby making it "countable" in some sense.

Ex 2) *The music of that nation is still in need of catching up with more modern music.*

Again, *the* is used in front of an uncountable noun music because you have a qualifying phrase *of that nation*.

5.2.3.4 *The* for Other Special Cases

There are cases in which *the* is always used.

- *The* + adjective: the rich (=the rich people), the poor (=the poor people), the wealthy (=the wealthy people), the sick (=the sick people), etc.

- *The* + a superlative + a noun: *the* best (*the* greatest, *the* most beautiful, *the* most wonderful, etc.) thing/person.

- Double comparatives:

  Ex 1) *The more, the better. The more quickly you do the job, the more likely you will get promoted.*

For the basic structure, refer to Double Comparatives. (section 10.6)

- [*One of the, some of the, several of the, most of the, all of the*] + [uncountable nouns or plural countable nouns]:

> *Ex 2)* <u>*One of the*</u> *most important people,* <u>*some of the*</u> *art,* <u>*several of the*</u> *dogs,* <u>*most of the*</u> *furniture,* <u>*most of the*</u> *churches,* <u>*all of the*</u> *students*

Refer to 5.3.4.

- Unique nouns that are not proper nouns: *the earth, the moon, the sun, the world, the universe, the air* (the space above the ground or around things), *the East, the West, the South, the North, the day, the night, etc.*

Q: Correct the following sentence(s).

Art of North Korea demonstrates one of best examples of irony: The poorer a nation becomes, greater its art becomes.

5.2.4 Usage with No Article

5.2.4.1 When a Countable Noun Is Used for Its Normal Purpose

> *Ex 1)* *She did not go to* <u>*school*</u> *yesterday.* (which specific school she did not go to is not important)

> *Ex 2)* *She did not go to* <u>*the school*</u>. (the specific school that the listener knows)

When a noun is used for its normal purpose and when it is not important to know which specific thing/institution/person is being referred to, you don't use any article.

Some examples of the phrases involving these are *go to school, go to church, go to prison, go to market, go to mall, go to bed, stay in hospital* (*school, church,* etc.), etc.

☞ <u>*Note*</u>: An article is not used only when you are talking about the noun with its general and normal purpose in mind. However, this usage is limited to very frequently used nouns (for example, "I went to bar" or "I went to classroom" would not work).

5.2.4.2 Other Idiomatic Expressions

- *day and night, day after day, from start to finish,* etc.
- *by car, by bus, by plane, by water, by land,* etc.
- *at home, at work, at night, at first, at last,* etc.

5.2.4.3 Kind(s)/Sort(s)/Type(s) Of

Ex 1)   *There is only one kind/sort/type of book/advice I can offer. That is the kind/sort/type of question/damage I cannot put up with.*

Ex 2)   *The SAT has several kinds/sorts/types of math problems.*

Ex 3)   *Many kinds/sorts/types of information will be given out in that convention.*

As Ex 1 shows above, for a singular countable noun, you have to use *kind* or *sort* or *type* in front of it. You use *kinds/sorts/types* in front of a plural countable noun (Ex 2). For an uncountable noun, you can use both *kind/sort/type* and k*inds/sorts/types* (Ex 1 and Ex 3).

☞ **Note**: In colloquial speech, you can use *kind/sort of* in a different sense.

Ex 4)   *We sort/kind of danced there, but other friends kind/sort of chatted with one another.*

When *kind/sort of* is used in this context, it simply conveys an attitude of uncertainty, hesitation, and a lack of passion.

Q: Correct the following sentence(s).

The only kind of an animal that hunts at the night in this forest is the owl based on the evidence of several kinds of dead insect normally eaten by the owl.

5.3 Ways to Express Quantity

5.3.1 To Modify Countable Nouns

- Singular: *one, another, each, every; a couple of, a pair of.*

> Ex 1)   *One (Each, Every) person needs to report to the*
> *authority.*

> Ex 2)   *A pair of pants is good enough for the little rascal.*

Notice that *a pair of* and *a couple of* come with plural nouns but are followed by a singular verb.

- Plural (in an increasing number): *two, both; three, four, five, etc.; few, a few, several; many, a large/great number of, numerous, countless,* etc.

> Ex 3)   *A large number of (or any of the above adjectives) spe-*
> *cies are found in the Antarctic.*

Notice that a plural verb is used in the plural case above.
A large number of is used like *many*.

☞ **Note**: [*The large/great number of*] + [a plural countable noun] must be considered singular and uses a singular verb because *the number,* not the plural noun after *of,* becomes the subject.

☞ **Note**: Unlike *a few, few* has a negative meaning in it. It *means not many*.

> Ex 4)   *Few (= not many) computers have this latest*
> *technology.*

5.3.2 To Modify Uncountable Nouns

- In order of increasing amount: *little, a little, much, a large/great amount/deal of,* etc.

> Ex 1)   *A large amount of (or any of the above adjectives) food*
> *is available for the winter this year.*

☞ **Note**: Just like *few, little* has a negative meaning in it. It means *not much*.

> Ex 2)   *Little* (= not much) *strength was left in him after that*
> *fight.*

5.3.3 To Modify Both Countable and Uncountable Nouns

- In order of increasing number or amount: *no, such, any/some, a lot of/lots of, other, plenty of, more, most, all,* etc.

  Ex 1)   _No_ (or _any, some, all, such_) _nation is_ in that alliance.

  Only *no, any, some, such* among these adjectives can also be used with singular countable nouns.

  Ex 2)   _No (or any of the above adjectives) nations are_ in that alliance.

  Ex 3)   _No (or any of the above adjectives) money is_ going to be allocated to that organization.

  ☞ **Note**: *any* used in this manner means *all* or *every kind of/all kinds of* whereas it means *no* when used in a negative sentence.

  Ex 4)   _You cannot_ have _any_ money. = *You can have no money.*

  Any used in a question means *some.*

  Ex 5)   *Did you see any (some) lawyer here?*

5.3.4 Using Of ({Some Expressions of Quantity} + *Of* + *{The, Possessive Nouns/Pronouns, Or This/That/These/Those}*)

  Ex 1)   _All_ (of the) _houses_ in that zone _are_ likely to be used commercially.

  Ex 2)   _Much_ (of the) _money is_ already wasted.

The expressions of quantity that fall into this category are *all, almost all, a few, a little, any, both, each, either, neither, one/two/three, none, several, some, most, many* or *much,* etc. As you saw from the previous sections, you can omit the parenthesized *of the,* but the meaning changes slightly when you use this construction; by adding *of* + *the* to these expressions of quantity, you basically restrict your choices to those **specific** people or things. Refer to section 4.9 for related concepts.

In addition to *the*, you can also put possessive pronouns/nouns (*my, your, his, her, its, our, their*, and *one's*) or other determiners such as *this, that, these*, and *those*.

> *Ex 3)*   *Several* (of my) *books are more than $100.*

> *Ex 4)*   *Most* (of those) *classes are easy to pass.*

Q: Correct the following sentence(s).

A great number of deer is found in that region but none of them is found in this region because a few large tiger is reported to appear here and because the number of carnivorous bears are increasing.

5.4   Expressing Order

5.4.1 Numerical Order

> *Ex 1)*   *Your attorney is in room fifty on the fifth floor.*

There are ordinal numbers such as *first, second, third, fourth*, etc. and cardinal numbers such as *one, two, three*, etc. As the example above shows, there are two ways to express numerical order.

[The] + [Ordinal Number] + [Singular Countable Noun]
Or
[Singular Countable Noun] + [Cardinal Number]

☞ *Note*: There are some nouns that are usually used with cardinal numbers but not with ordinal numbers. Nouns such as *track, flight, gate, concourse, room*, etc. belong to this group.

> *Ex 2)*   *Please go to gate 33 in concourse 3.*

However, when talking about its relative position, you can use ordinal numbers. For example, the following usage is okay.

> *Ex 3)*   *Go to the third room* (*track, gate*, etc.) *on the right there!*

5.4.2 (One, Another, The Other) and (Some, Other, The Other)

Refer to Consecutive Order (section 4.7)

5.5 Reason and Result (*So/Such/Too*)

Ex 1)   *The handyman was <u>so late</u> <u>that</u> we had to make another appointment.*

Ex 2)   *That was <u>so riveting a movie</u> <u>that</u> nobody in the audience was bothered by any noise made by the indecent couple.*

Ex 3)   *The statement he made was <u>such a controversial proposal</u> <u>that</u> the committee members were all disconcerted.*

Ex 4)   *They are <u>such mischievous children</u> <u>that</u> nobody wants to baby-sit them.*

So and *such* are used to indicate the reason for the occurrence expressed in the subsequent *that* clause. You can use only *so*, not *such* when only an adjective comes after it. When a noun as well as an adjective comes after it, you can use both.

Ex 5)   *The message was <u>too banal for us to keep</u> listening.*
        ≈*The message was <u>so banal that we could not keep</u> listening.*

[*Too*] + [adjective] + [infinitive] = [*so*] + [adjective] + [that ~ can/could not]

When it is *too* + *adjective* + *a/an* + *noun*, you change the *so/such* phrase accordingly.

For the usage of *so* and *such* without a subsequent *that* clause and the usage of *too*, refer to Word Order for Phrases Starting with So, As, How, Too and Such, Quite, What (section 5.2.2)

5.6 Using Hyphens

> *Ex 1)* *He is a very <u>well-known</u> director who made many <u>three-hour-long</u> epic movies.*

There are several ways to express compound words: writing the words separately, attaching them as one word without spaces between them, and attaching them with hyphens. There is not yet a consensus as to how to write compound words, but in many cases, using hyphens is recommended.

- Use hyphens to join two or more words that constitute an adjectival phrase **before a noun:**

  > *Ex 2)* *a <u>greatly-admired</u> leader, a <u>well-covered</u> subject, the <u>electricity-producing</u> device, a <u>long-lasting</u> impression, a <u>short-term</u> plan, the <u>most-exciting-show-of-the-year</u> award, etc.*

- Use hyphens for compound adjectives that contain numbers and **come before a noun:**

  > *Ex 3)* *the <u>one-hundred-ten-year-old</u> lady, a <u>forty-five-degree</u> angle, the new <u>eight-cylinder</u> Viper, five <u>one-hundred-dollar</u> bills, etc.*

☞ **Note**: You have to use a singular noun for the unit when using hyphens in this way (i.e., *year,* not *years, degree,* not *degrees,* etc.)

☞ **Note**: As you can see from the two cases above, compound adjectives are hyphenated **only when they come before a noun.**

  > *Ex 4)* *I am <u>twenty six years old.</u> (as contrasted with "I am a <u>twenty-six-year-old</u> bachelor.")*

- Use hyphens to discriminate between two homographs (the words with the same letters but different meanings) or to help more easily understand words with a confusing sequence of letters:

  > *Ex 5)* *re-sign* (as contrasted with *resign* which means *leave a job*), *pool-like* (as contrasted with *houselike,* etc. because two adjoined l's are somewhat awkward), *etc.*

- Other customary cases:

  > *Ex 6)* *anti-Semitism* (when combining with a capitalized words), *ex-wife, self-centered, semi-circle* (or *semicircle*), *pre-historic* (or *prehistoric*), *etc.*

> **Q: Correct the following sentence(s).**
>
> *That CEO made many multi-millions deals last year when the company was only five-years-old.*

5.7 Predicate Adjective

Ex 1) *The lion <u>was asleep</u> and <u>alone</u> when the hyenas took away the antelope that <u>was no longer alive</u>.*

There are certain adjectives that cannot be used to modify the following nouns but are used only as subjective complements (i.e., as predicate adjectives). Such adjectives usually start with the prefix *a-* : *afraid, alike, alive, alone, aloof, asleep, awake*, etc.

Ex 2) *The <u>golden</u> calf was destroyed and pulverized, and the <u>main</u> and <u>sole</u> reason for that is God's <u>eventual</u> wrath.*

There are also adjectives that cannot be used as predicate adjectives but only as the modifiers of nouns. Such adjectives include *chief, elder, eldest, eventual, former, golden, indoor, inner, main, major, mere, minor, only, outdoor, outer, primary, principal, sheer, sole, upper, utter*, etc.

> **Q: Correct the following sentence(s).**
>
> *The alike boys who were chief became principal.*

5.8 Adjectival Phrases With Prepositions

Ex 1) *Because the dying king was <u>proud of</u> his obedient sons, he was totally <u>content with</u> the existing state of his kingdom.*

There are some idiomatic adjectival phrases that normally use specific prepositions with them.

- **Of:** *afraid of, ashamed of, aware of, capable of, conscious of, certain of, confident of, desirous of, envious of, fond of, full of, guilty of, independent of, jealous of, nervous of* (or *nervous about*), *proud of, short of, sure of, tired of*, etc.

- **For:** *famous for, notorious for, ready for, responsible for*, etc.

- **From:** *absent from, different from, safe from*, etc.

- **To:** *contrary to, junior to, inferior to, prior to, senior to, similar to, superior to, oblivious to, due to*, etc.

☞ _**Note**_: In formal writing, _because of_ is used as an adverb whereas _due to_ is used as an adjective.

> _Error 1) He abhors his stepmother due to her hypocritical demeanor._

This colloquial use of _due to_ is, strictly speaking, ungrammatical because it is used as an adverbial phrase instead of an adjectival phrase.

> _Corr 1)_ _He abhors his stepmother because of her hypocritical_
>   _demeanor._

> _Ex 2)_ _His failing the important exam was due to his mother's death_
>   _a week ago._

Here, _due to_ is used correctly as an adjectival phrase in the subjective complement's place.

- **With:** _bored with, consistent with, content with, wrong with, popular with_, etc.

- **On:** _based on, dependent on, contingent on_, etc.

> _**Q: Correct the following sentence(s).**_
>
> _The castle is famous of its strong structure and similar with the newly built fortress, so the king was very desirous for possessing it._

☞ _**Note**_: Refer to 2.3.3 for the idioms using a [past participle + preposition] structure.

5.9 Order of Adjectives

> _Ex 1)_   _I know a gorgeous, tall, curvaceous, young, blond, Korean, Christian, rock singer._

There are some conventional rules on the order of adjectives. Here are the order of adjectives and their examples:

1. Article or determiner: a/an, the, this, that, these, those, my (and all other possessive pronouns), Sang's, etc.

2. Opinion Adjectives: nice, handsome, beautiful, diligent, etc.

3. Size Adjectives: tall, short, wide, narrow, long, short, big, small, etc.

4. Shape: triangular, linear, regular, oval, elliptical, rectangular, etc.

5. Age: young, old, teenage, antiquated, middle-aged, etc.

6. Color: red, orange, reddish, pale blue, bright red, etc.

7. Nationality: Korean, American, Chinese, Japanese, Taiwanese, French, British, etc.

8. Religion: Christian, Buddhist, Muslim, atheist, gentile, etc.

9. Material: iron, wood, metal, cotton, plastic, etc.

10. Nouns used as an adjective: <u>worship</u> service, <u>pep</u> rally, <u>inauguration</u> speech, etc.

11. The noun described by the adjectives.

Of course, enumerating multiple (more than four) adjectives to describe a noun as in Ex 1 is not recommended. You would rather do the following:

> *Ex 2)   I know a <u>blond</u> <u>Korean</u> <u>Christian</u> <u>rock</u> singer who is <u>gorgeous</u>, <u>tall</u>, <u>curvaceous</u>, and <u>young</u>.*

5.10 Adjectival Phrases and Clauses

5.10.1 Adjectival Phrases

> *Ex 1)   The 100-dollar chips <u>on the table</u> are earned by the guy <u>smoking that expensive Jamaican cigar.</u>*

The underlined phrases modify the nouns (*chips* and *guy*, respectively) in front of them and thus are, in their function, used as adjectives. As this example shows, prepositional phrases, participial phrases, and infinitival phrases can be used as adjectival phrases (or, of course, sometimes as adverbial phrases).

5.10.2 Adjectival Clauses

Refer to Relative Pronouns (Section 4.10).

5.11 Chapter Exam on Adjectives

Find all grammar errors and correct them most efficiently. The following sentences may contain one, multiple, or no error(s).

1) The Arabian was so a skilled artisan that he was capable to produce thousand-pounds metalwares.

2) An usual thing that he exhibited was such normal a habit that any asleep child can show.

3) Music of Hawaii is warm and blissful, but less full-time Hawaiian musicians live there due to the low pay they receive in that island.

4) You have to make the boy sit on chair and calm down; otherwise, he, ashamed for his wrongdoing, may do things that will hurt body.

5) A great number of beautiful swan is swimming on the lake; however, that ugly bird is also a kind of a swan and is not such different with the other kind.

6 Adverb

Adverbs, though not essential to the basic structure of the sentence, are very important because they add more accurate and detailed information to the sentence. Adverbs can add information about how, how often, how long, when, or where things are done.

6.1 Types of Adverbs

> *Ex 1)* *More specifically, when midnight was near, the extensively acclaimed actor very suddenly disappeared to take an uninterrupted rest through the night with his only greatly beloved woman, staying right next to her and not leaving her alone even for a single minute.*

The underlined words, phrases, and clauses have an adverbial function in the sentence. There are several common types of adverbs. Let us use the adverbs used in the example sentence above as examples:

- Natural adverbs: *very, not, alone, even*, etc.

- Adjective + ly: *specifically, extensively, suddenly, greatly*, etc.

- Prepositional phrase: *through the night, with his only greatly beloved woman, next to him, for a single minute*, etc.

- Infinitive phrase: *to take an uninterrupted rest*, etc.

- Participial phrase: *staying right next to her, never leaving her alone*, etc.

☞ *Note*: prepositional phrases, infinitive phrases, participial phrases, and clauses that start with an adverbial relative pronoun like *when* can also be used as adjectives if they are modifying the noun in front of them.

6.2 Roles of Adverbs

As you can see from Ex 1 of the previous section, adverbs have four major roles in a sentence:

- They modify verbs: *when the midnight was near, suddenly disappeared, not leaving*, etc.

- They modify adjectives: *extensively acclaimed, greatly beloved*, etc.

- They modify other adverbs: _very_ suddenly, _right_ next to her, _even_ for a single minute, etc.

- They modify the whole sentence: More _specifically,_ etc. Conjunctive adverbs (to be discussed in the next section) are most often used in this role of modifying the whole sentence.

6.3 Placement of Adverbs

Ex 1)   However, the congressmen have not yet seen the newly written agenda that the Speaker intends to discuss tonight.

The general rule for the order of adverbs is that adverbs should be as close to the word they modify as possible. When the adverb is simple and short, it usually comes before the modified word; when it is a long adverbial phrase or clause, it usually comes after the modified word as was the case with the adjectives. There are several rules that relate to this general rule:

- Conjunctive adverbs (such as _however, nonetheless, nevertheless, furthermore, moreover, thus, hence, accordingly, additionally, likewise,_ etc.) usually come at the beginning of the sentence. However, they can come right after the word that is being compared or contrasted.

Ex 2)   That country has several great professional sports leagues. Golf, nevertheless (Or Nevertheless, golf), doesn't have a pro league.

- Negative frequency adverbs (such as _never, rarely, scarcely, seldom,_ etc.) usually come right before the main verb; when there is an auxiliary verb, they come right after it.

Ex 3)   The giants have seldom seen such a tall dwarf.

☞ _Note_: If these negative adverbs appear at the beginning of a sentence for the emphasis of negative meaning, you have to invert the word order of the subject and the auxiliary verb. Refer to 6.6.

Ex 4)   Seldom have the giants seen such a tall dwarf

- Other frequency adverbs (such as _always, frequently, generally, normally, occasionally, often, sometimes, usually,_ etc.) can come either before or after an auxiliary verb depending on what you mean.

Ex 5)   I always cannot tolerate his behavior. (= I can never tolerate his behavior.)

Ex 6)   I <u>cannot</u> <u>always</u> *tolerate his behavior.* (= I can sometimes tolerate his behavior.)

☞ **Note:** The examples above clearly show the general interpretation method of this kind of adverb in a sentence: This kind of adverb modifies what comes after those adverbs, not before them. So *always* modifies *cannot tolerate* in Ex 6, and in Ex 7, *not* modifies *always tolerate*. The scope of modification of this kind of adverb is over the phrase that follows.

> *Q: Correct the following sentence(s).*
>
> *Never in the 100 years of my life I have seen such monsters; I have once seen, nevertheless, an ogre.*

6.4 Conjunctive Adverbs

There are many conjunctive adverbs or adverbial phrases that serve as transitions from one sentence or paragraph to another. These conjunctive adverbs can be categorized as follows:

- **Additive**: *additionally, also, analogously, moreover, furthermore, besides, in addition, likewise, similarly, in other words, for example, for instance, of course, as a matter of fact,* etc.

- **Causal**: *therefore, consequently, thus, hence, as a result, accordingly, otherwise, then,* etc.

- **Contrast**: *even so, however, instead, nevertheless, nonetheless, in contrast, on the contrary, on the other hand, rather, regardless, still, though, yet,* etc.

- **Dismissal**: *anyway, anyhow, in any case, at any rate,* etc.

- **Sequential:** *next, first, second, finally, in conclusion, as a recapitulation* (or *recap*), *subsequently,* etc.

> *Q: Correct the following sentence(s).*
>
> *He is fat, and beside, he is senile; nonetheless, all of his friends whom he hangs out with are criminals.*

6.5 Adverb-Related Diction

There are some adverbs that are error-prone and need emphasizing.

6.5.1 Late, Hard, Fast

Ex 1)   *You will lose the privilege if you come <u>late</u>.*

Ex 2)   *You will lose the prerogative if you don't work <u>hard</u>.*

Ex 3)   *You will lose the special right if you don't act <u>fast</u>.*

Late, hard, and *fast* can be used as both adjectives and adverbs. Understand that *lately* means *recently*, and *hardly* means *almost not at all*. There is no such word as *fastly*.

6.5.2 So, Such, Too, Quite

Refer to Section 5.2.2 Word Order for Phrases Starting with So, As, How, Too and Such, Quite, What and section 5.5 Reason and Result (So/Such/Too)

6.5.3 Hardly and Scarcely

Ex 1)   *The carpenter could <u>hardly</u> mend the house.*

Ex 2)   *The king <u>scarcely</u> avoided being murdered.*

Remember *hardly* and *scarcely* have a negative meaning within themselves, so you should not use another negative word such as *not, never,* or *nothing*, etc. with *hardly* and *scarcely*; if you do, you are making the serious 'Double Negatives' error.

6.5.4 Once and While

Ex 1)   <u>*Once*</u> *a respected scholar of the nation, the CEO has no desire to work in the academia now.*
      ≈ *Even though he was a respected scholar of the nation one time in the past, the CEO has no desire to work in the academia now.*

Ex 2)   <u>*While*</u> *a respected scholar of the nation, the president was also one of the most prolific writers in the academia.*
      ≈ *While he was a respected scholar of the nation, the president was one of the most prolific writers in the academia.*

Once is usually an adverb and means *at one time in the past* but in Ex 1, it carries the prepositional meaning "even though at one time he was." *While* is similar in meaning to *when*; in other words, *while* is not an adverb but a conjunction. Ex 2 shows another example of elliptical clause starting with *while*: refer to Participial Phrase and Dangling Participial Phrases for more.

☞ **Note**: *when* cannot replace *while* in the first sentence in Ex 2 because *when* cannot just have a noun after it; however, it can replace *while* in the second sentence in Ex 2.

6.5.5 Enough

Ex 1)   *There are <u>enough</u> <u>clergymen</u> in our parish.*

Ex 2)   *This mp3 player is <u>small</u> <u>enough</u> for my use.*

Enough can be used as either an adjective or an adverb. Ex 1 is an example in which *enough* is used as an adjective, and Ex 2 is an example in which *enough* is used as an adverb. The important thing to know is that *enough* has to come immediately after the adjective it modifies. When *enough* modifies a noun, it usually comes before it, but to put it after the noun is not ungrammatical.

6.5.6 Yet

Yet has different meanings depending on its position in the sentence or on the word it modifies.

Ex 1)   *has not <u>yet</u> recovered.* (not until now)

  I would rather that she did not recover <u>yet</u>. (not now but maybe later)

  <u>Yet</u>, she can still recover. (nevertheless or but)

  She can recover <u>yet</u> once again. (still)

☞ **Note**: *Yet* is also one of the coordinating conjunction, so it can connect two independent clauses. Refer to So, For, Yet, Nor (section 8.1.4)

Q: Correct the following sentence(s).

This book has not scarcely added anything to my old book that is enough compact to read really fastly.

6.6 Inversion

6.6.1 There/Here

Ex 1) *There are a math class and an English class for you to take.*

Ex 2) *Here is what you have requested for your granddaughter-in-law.*

There and *here* are adverbs and the verb that comes after them must agree with the subject that follows. Again, this switch of the usual word order is called **inversion**.

☞ *Note*: When a sentence is inverted, you have to be careful to match the verb with the true subject that comes after it. In particular, you have to be cautious about the compound subject that comes after the verb (as in Ex 1).

6.6.2 Negative Adverb Emphasis

Ex 1) *Never have I seen such love.*
≈ *I have never seen such love.*

Ex 2) *Not until the result of the test came out was she able to sleep.*
≈ *She was not able to sleep until the result of the test came out.*

When a negative adverb (such as *never, not until~, not only, hardly, scarcely, seldom, little, under no conditions, under no circumstances*, etc.) comes in the front of the sentence, the auxiliary verb comes before the subject.

☞ *Note*: When the main verb is an intransitive verb, you do not have to use an auxiliary verb for this kind of inverted sentence.

6.6.3 Adverbial Phrase Emphasis

Ex 1) *Among the huge number of wild rioters stands a vulnerable little girl*

Ex 2) *Beyond the reckoning of human mind does God work miracles.*

Even if the adverb or the adverbial phrase is not negative, you may invert the sentence for the emphasis of the adverb or the adverbial phrase.

☞ **_Note_**: Again, as Ex 1 shows, when the main verb is an intransitive verb, you do not have to use an auxiliary verb for this kind of inverted sentence

6.6.4 So/Neither/As

Ex 1) *My legs <u>are</u> hurting a lot after the toil, and <u>so are</u> my <u>arms</u>.*

≈ *My legs are hurting a lot after the toil, and my arms are hurting, too*

Ex 2) *My apprentices <u>left</u> me, and <u>so did</u> my <u>coworker</u>.*

≈ *My apprentices left me, and my coworker left me, too.*

Ex 3) *My parents <u>never denied</u> being Christians, and <u>neither did</u> my <u>siblings</u>.*

≈ *My parents never denied being Christians, and my siblings didn't, either*

Ex 4) *She <u>has</u> never experienced such a thing, and <u>neither have I</u>.*

≈ *She has never experienced such a thing, and I have not, either.*

[*So/Neither*] + [an auxiliary verb] + [Subject] is the pattern for this kind of inversion. The auxiliary verb must agree with its subject and the verb used in the preceding clause.

Ex 5) *The prisoners <u>will</u> like the preacher, <u>as will</u> <u>the warden</u>.*

As indicates that the manner in which (or the degree to which) *the prisoners* and *the warden* liked *the preacher* is identical.

Ex 6) *<u>So beautiful was the day</u> that nobody wanted to stay home.*

[*So*] + [adjective] can come at the beginning of the sentence and invert it.

6.6.5 Other Inversion Cases

Ex 1) *<u>Only if you finish your homework</u>, <u>will</u> I allow you to eat.*

Sentences that start with only (for example, *only if~, only by~, only after~, only before~, only when~,* etc.) are normally inverted.

> *Ex 2)* <u>*Great*</u> *is* <u>*our God*</u> *and* <u>*blessed*</u> <u>*are*</u> <u>*those*</u> *who are persecuted because of righteousness.*

When adjectives come at the beginning of the sentence and are emphasized, the sentence has to be inverted.

Q: Correct the following sentence(s).

There was a great number of people in the mall in which the Santa Claus was shouting, "Never again I will come here with so many gifts, and neither any other person has."

6.7 Adverbial Phrases and Clauses

6.7.1 Adverbial Phrases

The most common adverbial phrases are as follows:

- Prepositional phrases: phrases that contain a preposition and its object

  > *Ex 1)* <u>*Among the most important factors of his success*</u> *is his inviolable persistence* <u>*in times of*</u> <u>*hardship*</u>.

- Participial phrases: phrases that start with a participle (either a present or a past participle).

  > *Ex 2)* <u>*Having scrutinized the implied intention of the founding fathers in the constitution,*</u> *the Supreme Court Justices finally came to their final decision.*

- Infinitive phrases:

  > *Ex 3)* <u>*To study harder,*</u> *Gabriella removed all possible distractions.*

☞ **Note**: These phrases can also be used as adjectives when they modify the nouns before them. Refer to Adjectival Phrases (5.10.1)

6.7.2 Adverbial Clauses

Adverbial clauses usually start with subordinate conjunctions such as *when, where, because, as, if, after, before, so that,* etc.

> *Ex 1)* <u>When the jury couldn't decide whether the defendant was guilty or not,</u> *the judge had to intervene and give his opinion* <u>so that some of the jury on the fence could decide.</u>

☞ **_Note_**: Again, these subordinate clauses that start with these subordinate conjunctions could be used as nouns or adjectives. Refer to Special Questions, Interrogatives, and Indirect Questions (2.10.2), Nominal Clauses (3.7.2), and Relative Pronouns (4.10)

6.8 Chapter Exam on Adverbs

Find all grammar errors and correct them most efficiently. The following sentences may contain one, multiple, or no error(s).

1) The president hates people who are not on time; furthermore, his chief spokesperson came to the meeting lately.

2) The trumpeter has played never the trombone and is very un-skilled with it; yet, not until we find a professional trombonist he will stop playing it.

3) Between a huge dragon and a colossal giant does a vulnerable little girl who is less than four feet tall and a shabby dog stand.

4) My essays are marked by brevity, and so do my poems; only when I become an inefficient person I will start writing lengthier essays and poems.

5) Wonderful is the woman who gave birth to the child and the man who gladly took the child as his own; not many people will hardly become ungrateful for their sacrifice.

7 Preposition

Prepositions are words that show relations such as time, location, direction, cause, manner, etc. Prepositions are very important; as a matter of fact, in terms of frequency, the preposition *of* ranks second only to *the*, and the prepositions *to, in, for, on, with, as, by,* and *at* rank 4th, 6th, 12th, 13th, 17th, 18th, 19th, and 20th respectively in frequency ranking according to WORDCOUNT.ORG. A preposition always has to have an object called the object of the preposition, and only nouns or pronouns may serve as the objects of prepositions. A preposition and its object together constitute the prepositional phrase. A prepositional phrase functions as an adjective or adverb.

7.1 Preposition vs Adverb vs Conjunction

Before studying the basic usages of prepositions, let's understand the differences among prepositions, adverbs, and conjunctions.

Ex 1)   *you learn this technique before?* (adverb)

Ex 2)   *What did you do before you came to the U.S.A.?* (conjunction)

Ex 3)   *did you do before this career?* (preposition)

There are many words that can be used as a preposition, an adverb, or a conjunction. When a word modifies a verb, it is obviously an adverb as in Ex 1. The word that starts a subordinate clause is a conjunction. Only when there is a nominal phrase or a nominal clause acting as its object is the word a preposition. There are words that can be used only as prepositions or adverbs (such as *besides, inside, near, outside*, etc.), words that can be used only as prepositions or conjunctions (such as *as, for, since, till, until*, etc.), and words that can be used as all three of them (such as *after, before*, etc.)

Ex 4)   *This is the technique I wanted to talk about.*

Sometimes the object of the preposition does not appear right after the preposition as in Ex 4 (the object of the preposition *about, the technique,* appears in the front). This preposition-object inversion can occur in clauses beginning with an objective relative pronoun (often, the objective relative pronoun is omitted), in special questions (questions starting with interrogatives), in infinitive clauses and phrases, and in passive voice constructions.

7.2 Basic Uses of Prepositions

Before studying the basic usages of prepositions, let's understand the differences among prepositions, adverbs, and conjunctions.

7.2.1 Place

> *Ex 1)*   *I live at <u>9191 Heavens Avenue</u> in <u>Duluth, Georgia</u> <u>in the U.S.A.</u>*

> *Ex 2)*   *My friend lives <u>on Fifth Avenue</u> <u>in New York.</u>*

You have to use different prepositions for different locations or places. Some of the most common location prepositions are as follows:

- **In**: used for a place that is enclosed or within boundaries, such as a district (for example, *borough, city, county, province, state, country*), park, room, etc.

> *Ex 3)*   *There are beautiful Korea towns <u>in Gwinnett County, GA.</u>*

- **On:** used for a place that is on top of another place such as street and street name (for example, *Road, Street, Avenue, Boulevard, Drive*, etc.), coast, river, a type of transportation (for example, *a train, an airplane, a ship, a boat*; for a car, you use "in a car" instead of "on a car"), etc.

> *Ex 4)*   *My protégé used to live <u>on the West Coast</u> <u>on the Han River.</u>*

- **At:** used for a specific place or any location that starts with a number.

> *Ex 5)*   *My apprentices live <u>at 777 Blackstone Avenue</u> and study <u>at the University of Chicago</u>*

☞ **_Note_**: The difference between *in* and *at* is that *in* is used for a place within or inside a place whereas *at* is used for a specific place without the meaning of "inside" or "within the boundary of."

> *Ex 6)*   *I saw him <u>at the mall</u> and he was studying <u>at the food court</u> <u>in the main building</u>*

- Others: There are numerous prepositions that are used for a place: *aboard, about, above, across, against, around, behind, below, beneath, beside, between, by, in front of, inside, near, outside, over, under, underneath, within,* etc. Refer to a nice dictionary for their exact usages and meanings.

7.2.2 Time and Duration

Ex 1) *My grandson was married in January of 1999 on the third Saturday at 5:00 pm.*

Ex 2) *They were married on the fourth of July, 1999 and divorced on July fourth, 2000.*

In is used for a year, month, or season; *on* is for a date or day; *at* is for a specific time.

Ex 3) *I can do this job in three hours. I have studied this subject for three years since the winter three years ago. During that winter, I recuperated from the mental trauma.*

In could be used for duration. *For, since*, and *during* are also used for duration; refer to Present Perfect (Have/Has + Past Participle) (2.2.3) *For* is usually used with a phrase expressing an action that occurs continuously over a designated time period; therefore, the verb it modifies is in the perfect tense. *During* is used with a phrase expressing an activity that is somewhat intermittent (the activity during the time is on and off, not necessarily continuously) and is, therefore, modifies a verb in the simple past tense.

Error 1) During a day, during two years, etc.

Corr 1) During the day, during the summer, during the lecture, etc.

Ex 4) *I stayed in the seminar from 5:00 pm to 10:00 pm.*

Even though *from~ to~* indicates a duration or a specific time frame, you normally use the simple tense instead of the perfect tense.

7.2.3 Direction

Ex 1) *Paul went to the lake, walked toward(s) the water line, dove into the cold water, but instead fell onto the lake floor.*

To is used for a specific direction and *toward(s)* is used for a general direction. *Into* is used to emphasize a movement to the interior of something; *onto* is used to emphasize a movement toward the surface of something.

> *Ex 2)*   *I am looking forward to seeing your beautiful eyes. I object to your going to that college.*

As was said before, you need to be able to distinguish preposition *to* from *to* that makes an infinitive, and if it is a preposition, you have to use a gerund instead of an infinitive.

> *Ex 3)*   *You have to take the train bound for Atlanta.*

For could be used for a destination; most of the time, it is used in this idiomatic expression, *bound for*.

7.2.4 Cause and Purpose

> *Ex 1)*   *Because of your noble act, we all became different people for our country.*

> *Ex 2)*   *His debacle was due to his adamant heart.*

Because of is a preposition indicating a cause; however *because* is used only as a conjunction. *Due to* is also used to indicate a cause.

☞ *Note*: In formal writing, a *because of* phrase is used as an adverb whereas a *due to* phrase is used as an adjective. Refer to Adjectival Phrases With Prepositions (5.8).

For can also be a preposition indicating a purpose or a conjunction indicating a cause or a reason. Refer to So, For, Yet, Nor (8.1.4).

☞ *Note*: : In formal writing, when you want to indicate a purpose as an adverb, **avoid using [for] + [gerund]; instead, use [to] + [infinitive]**.

7.2.5 Manner

> *Ex 1)*   *Did you come here by train or by airplane?*

> *Ex 2)*   *The dictionary was written by the most famous lexicographers.*

By indicates the manner in which an action is done or the agent by whom the action is done.

> *Ex 3)* <u>*As the final decision-maker,*</u> *he had to choose* <u>*the same*</u> *decision* <u>*as*</u> *the one before.*

As indicates a title, a qualification, or a comparison.

7.2.6 Other Less Frequently Used Prepositions

A decent dictionary is likely to list hundreds of prepositions. Let me give a small list of prepositions that are not as frequently used as the ones in the previous subsections but still important:

according to, across, ahead of, all over, alongside, amid/amidst, as of (≈ starting from ~), as to (≈ as for ~, about ~), aside, astride (≈ one leg on each side of ~), away from, bar (≈ except), barring (≈ except the case of ~), beyond, circa (≈ about the time of ~), concerning, considering, except, excepting, excluding, failing, given, in place of, in view of, including, less (≈ minus ~), notwithstanding, on top of, opposite, other than, past, pending (≈ while waiting ~), per, plus, regarding, save (≈ except), saving, thanks to, throughout, up to (≈ as much as ~, as many as ~, or to the power of ~), versus, via (≈ through), etc.

> *Q: Correct the following sentence(s).*
>
> *Due to his small lie, he was forced to give up his position in the fifth day of January by the honesty-loving citizens; for becoming an official in that nation, one must be completely frank and open except national security requires confidentiality.*

7.3 Prepositions vs Particles

> *Ex 1)* *I drove* <u>*up*</u> *the hill.* <u>*Up*</u> *the hill I drove.* (preposition)

> *Ex 2)* *I gave* <u>*up*</u> *the effort. I gave it* <u>*up*</u>. (particle)

These two examples show the differences between a preposition and a particle. A particle is a part of a phrasal verb and is indistinguishable from preposition in its form. **A phrasal verb is basically an idiom that consists of a verb and a particle(s)** such as *add up, ask out, back off, back up, blow up, break down, break up, bring up, call back, call off, carry out, catch up,* *check out, cheer up, chicken out, cross out, cut off, do over, fill in, fill out, find out, give away, give up, hold back, keep out, look up, make up, pass away, pay back, put down, set up, sort out, switch off/on, take apart, take back, take out, think over, turn off/on/down, try on, wake up,* etc. For the meanings of these phrasal verbs, refer to a good dictionary that includes idioms or a comprehensive list of phrasal verbs. These phrasal verbs form single semantic units (i.e., the verb part and the particle cannot be separated). However, prepositions are independent of the verbs and do not affect their meanings; thus, you can move the prepositional phrase to the front of the sentence, separating it from the verb as Ex 1 shows. On the other hand, moving a particle from a phrasal verb results in ungrammaticality (In Ex 2, *Up the effort I gave* will not make any sense).

☞ **Note**: As some of the above-mentioned phrasal verbs show, some phrasal verbs act as intransitive verbs (i.e., they do not require an object). Therefore, unlike prepositions, particles do not require an object.

Ex 3)   The bully <u>chickened out</u> when he saw my formidable power.

Furthermore, for most phrasal verbs, if the object of a phrasal verb is a pronoun, it has to come between the verb and the particle.

Ex 4)   Can you <u>put off the meeting</u> for me? Can you <u>put the meeting off</u> for me?

Ex 5)   Can you <u>put it off</u> for me?

Here the phrasal verb *put off* (which means 'to postpone') needs to have its object *it* (or any simple objective pronoun such as *me, you, him, her, it, us, and them*) between *put* and *off*. *Put off it* is wrong.

> *Q: Correct the following sentence(s).*
>
> *She knows that he backed up her in the dispute, so she is going to ask out him confidently because she is convinced now that he is fond of her.*

7.4   Preposition-Related Diction

7.4.1 Verb-Related

Some verbs use different prepositions for different types of objects.

- **Agree**: *agree to* an offer, *agree with* a person, *agree on* a price or terms of a contract, and *agree in* principle.

- **Argue:** *argue about* a matter or issue, *argue with* a person, and *argue for/against* a proposition.

- **Compare:** *compare to* a similar thing (to show similarity) and *compare with* a different thing (usually to show differences).

- **Correspond:** *correspond to* a matter and *correspond with* a person.

There are some verbs that usually require only a certain preposition:

- **To***: accede to, adapt to, adhere to, belong to, conform to (or with), contribute to, happen to, immigrate to, listen to, look forward to, object to, proceed to, resort to, etc.*

☞ <u>Note</u>: Again, make sure that you understand that the *to*'s used in this way are prepositions, not the *to* in the infinitive, so you have to put a noun/pronoun after them

- **Of:** *accuse (someone) of, approve of, consist of, die of, get rid of, take advantage of, take care of, etc.*

- **From:** *adapt from, borrow (something) from, emigrate from, graduate from, infer (something) from, profit from, prohibit from, protect (something/someone) from, etc.*

- **With:** *comply with, concur with, deal with, proceed with, reason with, reward (someone) with, etc.*

- **On:** *concentrate on, focus on, depend on, impose (something) on, improve on, insist on, rely on, comment on, etc.*

- **In:** *believe in, engage in, participate in, specialize in, succeed in, excel in, etc.*

7.4.2 Noun-Related

- **In:** *belief in, interest in, participation in, success in, etc.*

- **For:** *appetite for, concern for, desire for, disdain for, fondness for, hope for, etc.*

- **From:** *protection from, separation from, etc.*

- **Of:** *appreciation of, approval of, grasp of, hatred of, understanding of, etc.*

- **On:** *commentary on, dependence on, reliance on, etc.*

- **To:** *addiction to, commitment to, devotion to, dedication to, objection to, contribution to,* etc.

- **With:** *association with, disappointment with, preoccupation with, satisfaction with, obsession with,* etc.

☞ *Note*: There are some SAT favorites such as ***preoccupation with, satisfaction with, commitment to, objection to, comply with, desire for***, etc.

7.4.3 Adjective-Related

Refer to Adjectival Phrases With Prepositions (5.8) and Passive Voice Using Other Prepositions than By (2.3.3)

7.4.4 Other Tricky Prepositions

There are some prepositions that need further explaining.

- **Among vs Between:** *Among* is used for three or more persons or things whereas *between* is used only for two persons or things.

- **Beside vs Besides:** *Beside* is used always as a preposition and means "next to." *Besides* can be used as a preposition meaning "in addition to," or as an adverb meaning "also" or "moreover."

- **Despite and In Spite Of:** These have the same meaning and indicate contradiction; conjunctive counterparts of these prepositions would be *though* or *although*.

- **Instead vs Instead Of:** *Instead of* is a preposition but *instead* is an adverb. To compare other parts of speech than nouns, you can use *rather than*.

> *Ex 1)* *You have to paint it <u>accurately</u> <u>rather than</u> <u>beautifully</u>, using <u>a pencil</u> <u>instead of</u> <u>a brush</u>.*

Q: Correct the following sentence(s).

The nurse who emigrated to the U.S. could not agree to the doctor despite of his great reputation; therefore, the doctor had to find another nurse who would concur to him and not object to follow his orders among the two remaining nurses available.

7.5 Omission of Prepositions

> *Ex 1)* *Because we did not meet <u>last Monday</u>, let's meet <u>next Sunday</u>.*
> *We couldn't agree <u>last time</u>, but <u>this time</u> we could reach an*
> *agreement.*

It is redundant to put preposition *on* in front of a nominal phrase consisting of a time noun (such as a day of the week or a time, etc.) modified by words such as *last, next, this, that,* etc. These phrases act as adverbial phrases without the help of prepositions.

> *Ex 2)* *The plastic surgeon was <u>busy talking</u> to the pretty nurse and seemed*
> *to have much <u>fun flirting</u> with female employees of the hospital*
> *while other doctors <u>had a tough time trying</u> to resuscitate dying*
> *patients.*

In these common phrases, you do not put preposition *in* in front of the ~ing (present participle).

7.6 Redundant Prepositions

> *Error 1) It is impossible to <u>kick him off of</u> the soccer team during this season.*

> *Corr 1) It is impossible to <u>kick him off</u> the soccer team in this season.*

People use a lot of superfluous preposition as Error 1 shows. In formal speech or writing, you have to avoid using these redundant words. Some of the most common errors of this type are underlined in the following examples:

- **Verb + preposition(s):** *dominate <u>over</u>, help <u>out</u> with, fry <u>up</u>, fall <u>down</u>, extract <u>out</u>, fight <u>against</u>, extend <u>out</u>, miss <u>out on</u>, kick off <u>of</u>, fill <u>up</u>, open <u>up</u>, protest <u>against</u>, meet <u>up with</u>, fall off <u>of</u>,* etc.

- **Other example sentences:** *Where did you go <u>to</u>? Where did you stay <u>in</u>? He threw the ball out <u>of</u> the door. Get inside <u>of</u> the house!*

In formal writing or speech, it is recommended that you do not use those underlined prepositions unless they give the intended non-redundant meaning. Refer to Repetition of words with the same meaning (section 12.1).

> *Q: Correct the following sentence(s).*
>
> *My husband and I will finally meet up on next Thursday and help my mother out with her home improvement project.*

7.7 Chapter Exam on Prepositions

Find all grammar errors and correct them most efficiently. The following sentences may contain one, multiple, or no error(s).

1) My assistant lived on 1200 Jimmy Carter Boulevard for 35 years; his preoccupation in living there differs with my obsession for living at Seoul.

2) The parents were looking forward to participate on the Christmas event, to be held in 5:00 p.m. at Atlanta, GA.

3) The evening in which his girlfriend agreed with his offer was in the same day as the morning on which her ex-boyfriend fell off of a long ladder and broke his legs.

4) Beside the biologist's great I.Q., her strong willpower also contributed on her winning the award between the three candidates.

5) The colonel said that for winning a battle, the soldiers have to have the desire of victory and the commitment on patriotism because they can only resort on one another.

8 Conjunction

Conjunctions are the words that connect parts of a sentence: They can connect clauses, phrases, or just words. There are three kinds of conjunctions: coordinating conjunction, subordinating conjunction, and correlative conjunctions.

8.1 Coordinating Conjunction

Coordinating conjunctions can connect independent clauses or phrases. There are seven coordinating conjunctions in English. You can remember them well by using an acronym BOYFANS: *But, Or, Yet, For, And, Nor*, and *So*.

8.1.1 And

> *Ex 1)* *The GOP will lose this election, and its range of influence will shrink. The Democratic Party and the President Elect will celebrate their victory.*

Conjunction and has several major functions:

- To connect two closely related independent clauses as in "I am a boy, and you are a girl."

- To state two statements which are chronologically sequential as in Ex 1.

- To state contrasting ideas (act like the conjunction but or yet) as in "He is a smart guy, and he still makes this mistake." However, this case is rarely used.

- To indicate a result of the first statement, which usually starts with an imperative as in "Clean your room, and you will not be punished!"

☞ *Note*: When you list more than two words using *and* or *or*, you may or may not attach a comma before *and*. Nowadays, however, more writers are starting to put a comma there to minimize confusion.

> *Ex 2)* *She is a mom, a wife, a teacher, and an entrepreneur.*

☞ **_Note_**: In formal writing, you put a comma before these coordinating conjunctions that start another independent clause, especially when the clauses are long.

8.1.2 Or

Ex 1) *The NFL can give the venal umpires a proper discipline, or it can lose a lot of football fans. The chairman can disqualify them or make them pay serious fines.*

Conjunction or has several major functions:

- To indicate that only one of the two possibilities can occur as in Ex 1.

- To indicate a result of not performing the first statement (often when *or* follows an imperative as in "Wash your face, or you will not be given food!")

- To indicate refinement or correction of the first clause as in "He is apathetic, or he at least seemed so when I met him."

- To list possible alternatives as in the second sentence of Ex 1.

8.1.3 But

Ex 1) *Any student can take this abstruse course, but he or she should not expect to receive a nice grade. All but the professor of that course are generous to the students in terms of grades.*

Conjunction but has several major functions:

- To indicate contrast between clauses as in Ex 1.

- To indicate an exception as in the second sentence of Ex 1. In this use, it means the same as "*except*." In this sense, but used in this way is a preposition rather than a conjunction.

- To be placed between two verbs that share the same subject to indicate contrast between those actions as in "He did not say it, but implied it."

8.1.4 So, For, Yet, Nor

> *Ex 1)* *I worked on this thesis very hard, <u>so</u> I deserve to get your compliment.*

So means "and therefore" when used as a conjunction.

> *Ex 2)* *She received the award, <u>for</u> her act was exceptionally amazing.*

For means "and the reason is that" when used as a conjunction.

> *Ex 3)* *I haven't eaten any meal, <u>yet</u> I feel very energetic and invigorated.*

Yet means "but nevertheless" when used as a conjunction. *Yet* has several meanings as an adverb. Refer to Yet (6.5.6)

> *Ex 4)* *He is not extremely prim, <u>nor</u> is he very unkempt.*
> ≈ He is not extremely prim, but he is not so unkempt, either.

Nor means "but ~ not ~ either" when used as a conjunction. Notice the inversion after *nor* when used in this way.

☞ **Note**: Conjunctions *so*, *for*, and *yet* are often used as adverbs or prepositions, so you need to be clear about their meanings and usages when they are used as adverbs. Refer to Preposition vs Adverb vs Conjunction (7.1) and Cause and Purpose (7.2.4).

☞ **Note**: One of the common errors in formal writing is the use of *and, but, or, nor,* and *for* after a semicolon (;) or a colon (:).

> *Error 1)* *The prime minister loved compliments; <u>but</u> the followers were stingy in giving him what he wanted.*

You may have a conjunctive adverb (section 6.4) after a semicolon.

> *Corr 1)* *The prime minister loved compliments; <u>however,</u> the followers were stingy in giving him what he wanted.*

And can be used after a semicolon in a rare case in which the semicolons act as "big" commas, separating groups, each of which contains several commas.

> *Ex 5)* *The three families that joined our party are the director's family consisting of the director, his wife, and his daughter; the main actor's family consisting of the actor, his wife, and his son; and the main actress's family consisting of the actress, her husband, and her two adopted sons.*

> *Q: Correct the following sentence(s).*
>
> *I do not like him, nor she does; and so we will not invite him to our dinner.*

8.2 Subordinating Conjunction

> *Ex 1)* *The suspect came to this ghetto because the police announced that he was at large and started searching for him with all their resources.*

Subordinating conjunctions connect a dependent clause to an independent clause. Some of the subordinating conjunctions are:

- **Time:** *after, as, as soon as, before, once, since, till, until, when, whenever, while,* etc.

- **Place:** *where, wherever,* etc.

- **Condition:** *as long as, even if, given (that), if, if only, in case (that), in the event (that), provided (that), when, whenever,* etc.

- **Reason:** *as, because, now that, since, so that, in order that, why,* etc.

- **Concession:** *although, even if, even though, while,* etc.

- **Manner:** *as, as if, as though,* etc.

- **Contrast:** *whereas, while,* etc.

When these are used as subordinating conjunctions, you have to have a dependent clause after them.

☞ **Note**: Sometimes when the subject and the verb part of the dependent clause are obvious, you can omit them. This is called **elliptical adverbial clauses** (refer to Participial Phrase (2.4.4)). This is related to participial phrase, and you have to be careful that you do not make a **dangling** phrase error (i.e., the omitted subject of the participle or noun must match the subject of the main clause).

> *Ex 2)* <u>*When*</u> *(the chemical is)* <u>*stimulated,*</u> *this chemical can explode.*

> *Ex 3)* *The CEO,* <u>*though*</u> *(she is)* <u>*very rich,*</u> *is really miserly.*

☞ **Note**: Many of the subordinating conjunctions can be used as adverbs or prepositions. Refer to Preposition vs Adverb vs Conjunction (7.1)

> ***Q: Correct the following sentence(s).***
>
> *While playing for the county football team, his legs were hurt because the excessively competitive atmosphere which made the athletes play recklessly.*

8.3 Correlative Conjunctions

Correlative conjunctions are conjunctions that pair up with other words to form a kind of compound conjunction. Some of the major correlative conjunctions are:

- **Both ~ And ~:**

  > *Ex 1)* *The world is becoming* <u>*both*</u> *more populated* <u>*and*</u> *more educated.*

- **Not Only ~ But Also ~:**

  > *Ex 2)* *This cosmetic surgery procedure is very popular* <u>*not only in Korea*</u> <u>*but also*</u> <u>*in America.*</u>

  > *Ex 3)* <u>*Not only*</u> *did he have to stop his negative campaign,* <u>*but*</u> *he* <u>*also*</u> *had to restructure his whole campaign strategy.*

  > *Ex 3B)* <u>*Not only*</u> *did* <u>*the justice*</u> <u>*not*</u> *come to my party,* <u>*but*</u> *he* <u>*also*</u> *did not invite me to his party.*

Notice the inversion and the word order after *but* in Ex 3 and the correct use of the extra *not* after *the justice* in Ex 3B.

- **Not ~ But ~:**

  > *Ex 4)* <u>*Not*</u> *the gaudy mini skirt* <u>*but*</u> *the tight blue jeans* <u>*were*</u> *what she wanted for her birthday.*

- **Either ~ Or ~:**

  > *Ex 5)* *The new supervisor can report* <u>*either to*</u> *the director of marketing* <u>*or to*</u> *the vice president.*

- **Neither ~ Nor ~:**

  Ex 6)   The workshop was <u>neither</u> didactic <u>nor</u> fun.

- **Whether ~ Or ~:**

  Ex 7)   I have to decide <u>whether</u> to apply to a law school <u>or</u> to start earning money.

  Refer to Nominal If/Whether Clause (3.7.2.3)

- **Just As ~ So Too ~ (or So):**

  Ex 8)   <u>Just as</u> your positive attitude <u>helped</u> your admission, <u>so too did</u> your great intelligence.

  Notice the inversion after *so too*.

- **~ As Well As ~:**

  Ex 9)   Econometrics uses Calculus <u>and</u> Linear Algebra <u>as well as</u> Statistics.

☞ *Note*: Notice that the sentence is complete before *as well as* in Ex 9. In other words, using "*Calculus, Linear Algebra, as well as Statistics*" instead is wrong. In this sense, *as well as* should be considered as leading a prepositional phrase meaning *in addition to*.

☞ *Note*: When correlative conjunctions *not only A but also B, not A but B, either A or B*, and *neither A nor B* are used in the subject's place, the main verb should agree in number and gender with **B**, which is closer in proximity to the verb. That is why this grammatical law is sometimes called **the law of proximity**. Refer to Ex 4. The law of proximity applies also to pronouns: The pronoun that is in the clause following these phrases and refers to these phrases has to agree in number and gender with **B**, even though in most cases you do not have to be this punctilious.

> *Q: Correct the following sentence(s).*
>
> *Not only she is brilliant, but also she is pretty; therefore, neither his parents or his sister are going to reject her as his bride.*

8.4 Parallelism

In formal English, parallelism is very important. **Parallelism means using the same grammatical structures or styles within or across phrases or sentences that list or express ideas of equal importance.**

*Error 1) The war in Afghanistan was <u>time-consuming, sanguinary,</u> and
<u>a costly one.</u>*

This sentence will sound smoother by the application of parallelism.

*Corr 1) The war in Afghanistan was <u>time-consuming, sanguinary,</u> and
<u>costly.</u>*

Because *time-consuming* and *sanguinary* are adjectives the last item of
the list must also be in an adjective form *costly*, not a nominal phrase *a
costly one.*

*Error 2) I could <u>neither believe</u> his words verbatim <u>nor could</u> doubt
them completely.*

To follow parallelism exactly, the above sentence should be corrected.

*Corr 2) I could <u>neither believe</u> his words verbatim <u>nor</u> doubt them
completely.*

The more similar in the structure or form the elements of the list are,
the better and smoother the sentence will sound. So for example, a
gerund phrase should be followed by a gerund phrase, not by an
infinitive phrase. Likewise, a nominal clause should be followed by
another nominal clause.

**Parallelism is especially important in structures containing
correlative conjunctions.** So the *A* and *B* in each correlative
construction given in <u>*Note*</u> at the end of section 8.3 must be identical
in grammatical structure, in keeping with the law of parallelism.

Q: Correct the following sentence.

*Her face was small in size, round in shape, and its color was ivory,
but to call her a classic beauty or ignoring her as a common face is
entirely up to you because not only your parents but also I are
going to object to your opinion.*

8.5   Chapter Exam on Conjunctions

Find all grammar errors and correct them most efficiently. The following
sentences may contain one, multiple, or no error(s).

1)   Both the fact that the man was a former felon and his wife's
     having been a famous swindler makes it difficult for the couple
     to live either in that high-class subdivision or the other opulent
     neighborhood.

2)   The pilots can get their training in not only the airfield but also
     in the simulation room in order that acquire their certificates.

3)   Just as the emperor was hailed in the whole empire, as too the
     governor did in his province.

4)   Neither the democrats who occupied more than 60 percent of
     the House or the Speaker of the House who had the President on
     his side were able to satisfy the citizens of the United States.

5)   The people of Korea, who are famous for their efficiency, the
     people of Japan, who are well-known for their service, the
     people of China, who are recognized for their productivity, as
     well as Americans, who are known widely to be creative, are
     competing for dominance in the world's export market.

9 Interjection

The last part of speech to be covered is interjection. Interjections are words used to express explicit emotion or to fill pauses. Literally, the word interjection means "the state of being thrown in between (words)," and this definition basically says almost everything about interjections. One characteristic of interjections is that it has no grammatical connection with other parts of the sentence.

9.1 Basic

Ex 1)   *Alas, all the people I love have passed away.*

Ex 2)   *Ouch! It hurts. Stop it!*

Ex 3)   *I would call her... um... a shrew!*

Ex 1 and Ex 2 show interjections that express explicit emotions whereas Ex 3 shows an interjection that simply fills a pause and expresses a moment of hesitation or thinking.

Here are some of the examples of interjections that usually express explicit emotion: *ah, aha, alas, bravo, cheers, damn, darn, duh, eh, ew, gee, gosh, grrr, ha, hello, hey, hi, hooray, hurrah, hurrah, oh, o, oops, ouch, ow, shh, uh, ugh, uh-huh, uh-uh, whew, whoops, wow, yes, yikes, yoo-hoo, yuk,* etc. For their respective meanings and usages, refer to a nice dictionary. These interjections usually come at the beginning of a sentence and end with an exclamation point (!).

Here are other examples of interjections used to fill a pause: *er, uh, um, umm,* etc. These interjections usually come with an ellipsis or ellipses.

9.2 Expletives

Ex 1)   *It is important to comply with his opinion.*

Ex 2)   *This cheesecake is damned delicious.*

Ex 3)   *Darn it! You did it again.*

The empty subject *it* is an expletive. I have pointed out in section 4.8 that expletives are words that have no semantic content (thus the term 'empty') as in Ex 1. *There/here* are expletives of this kind. Another definition of expletive is simply "bad language." Ex 3 shows an expletive that can be considered an interjection. The number of expletives is increasing; however, try not to use these "bad expletives" in formal writing unless you have to use them. Of course, there are genres of writing that make extensive use of expletives to achieve intended literary effects.

10   Comparison

Comparatives and superlatives are not parts of speech, but since we have completed chapters on parts of speech, let's study comparison-related grammar before we move to the part on style.

10.1 Basics

10.1.1 Comparatives

You use comparatives when you compare two things or two groups.

Ex 1)   Yao Ming is taller than Hongman Choi

Ex 2)   His daughter is more gorgeous than his girlfriend.

Ex 3)   Between the two candidates, Barak Obama is absolutely the less conservative guy (than the other guy).

You usually attach –er to adjectives that have only one syllable to make them comparatives. For adjectives ending with –e, you simple add –r (such as *wider, later,* etc.). If an adjective has two syllables ending with *y*, you attach –ier (such as *prettier, uglier, dirtier*, etc.) to make it a comparative. For all other cases of an adjective with more than one syllable, add more in front of the adjective to make it a comparative.

Ex 4)   The wizards can do the job more effectively than the trolls (do).

Ex 5)   The witches can do the trick faster than the elves (can).

For adverbs, you usually add more in front of it; however, there are adverbs such as *faster, harder, later*, etc. which simply takes the –er form.

10.1.2 Superlatives

You use superlatives when you compare three or more things or groups.

Ex 1)   According to many historians, King Solomon is considered the richest person who has ever lived.

Ex 2)   *Superman is thought to be <u>the mo'st powerful</u> superhero.*

Ex 3)   *<u>Among the republican nominees</u>, John McCain was <u>the most persistent maverick</u>.*

To make superlatives, you attach –est to one-syllable (monosyllabic) adjectives and most in front of more-than-one-syllable (multisyllabic) adjectives. Most of the time, you have to add *the* in front of these superlatives when they modify a countable noun.

Ex 4)   *The R&B singer can sing this song <u>most beautifully</u>.*

Ex 5)   *<u>Among the athletes</u> standing on the track, <u>the skinniest African</u> can run 100 meters <u>fastest</u>.*

You attach *most* in front of multisyllabic adverbs and –est in front of one-syllable adverbs such as *fastest*, *hardest*, etc. You normally do not attach *the* in front of a superlative adverb when that adverb does not modify an adjective which modifies a noun.

10.1.3 Expressing Superlatives Using Comparatives

Ex 1)   *That teaching assistant has been <u>more helpful</u> for this test <u>than any other person</u> has.*

    ≈ *That teaching assistant has been the most helpful person for this test.*

Ex 2)   *<u>No (other) teacher</u> was <u>more instructive than he</u>.*

    ≈ *He was the most instructive teacher among the teachers.*

Ex 3)   *The teacher had <u>never</u> been <u>prouder</u> of his students.*

    ≈*The teacher was prouder of his students than he had ever been before.*

☞ **Note**: Some people insist on using *more proud* for *prouder* even though *prouder* is more consistent with the general rules of making comparatives and superlatives.

10.1.4 Irregular Adjectives/Adverbs

> *Ex 1)* *The circumstances in his childhood were <u>worse</u> than I had imagined.*

There are adjectives and adverbs that take irregular forms when changed into comparatives and superlatives.

- Good   better   best
- Well   better   best

☞ *Note*: *Well* can be an adjective, meaning *healthy*, or it could be an adverb form of *good*.

- Bad   worse   worst
- Badly   worse   worst
- Far   farther/further   farthest/ furthest

☞ *Note*: *Far* can be used as both an adjective and an adverb. *Farther/the farthest* can indicate only physical distance whereas *further/the furthest* can mean a general advancement to a greater degree.

- Little less   least
  (Use *lesser* when you say the phrase *to a lesser degree*)
- Many   more   most
- Much   more   most
- Old   older/elder   oldest/the eldest

☞ *Note:* *Elder/the eldest* are used only for a member of a family whereas *older/the oldest* is for general use.

Q: Correct the following sentence.

The government's spending is more worse than its corruption; moreover, farther problems exist in Washington.

10.1.5 Absolute Adjectives/Adverbs

> *Error 1) To Jews and Christians, Jehovah is the <u>most unique</u> God among all gods.*

> *Corr. 1) To Jews and Christians, Jehovah is the <u>unique</u> God among all gods.*

There are some adjectives and adverbs that can be used neither as comparatives nor as superlatives because they indicate one and only one quality. The following adjectives and their adverb counterparts are thus called **absolute adjectives** and **absolute adverbs:** *absolute, complete, entire, fatal, final, ideal, impossible, indispensable, inevitable, optimal, supreme, ultimate, universal, unique,* etc.

☞ *Note*: *Superior/Inferior* are not used in comparatives (i.e., *more superior than/more inferior than* are not used because *more* is redundant and these adjectives are used with the preposition *to*, instead of *than*).

☞ *Note*: In a casual speech, people often use these absolute adjectives and adverbs in comparatives or superlatives, but in formal writing or speech, you have to avoid using these as comparatives or superlatives.

Q: Correct the following sentence.

I could have said a more ideal story that suits your taste, but this testimony is more absolute even though it seems more impossible to believe.

10.1.6 Illogical Comparison

Error 1) The weather in Korea during autumn is better than Hawaii.

Many learners make the error of **illogical comparison** in which the things being compared are not logically comparable: You generally cannot compare *the weather* with a place (*Hawaii*) unless you are making a metaphorical literary expression. Almost all of the time, the things that are being compared in a sentence must be logically comparable; in other words, they have to be in the same category. So the sentence above must be revised into the following sentence.

Corr. 1) The weather in Korea during autumn is better than that in Hawaii.

The underlined word *that* in the sentence above refers to *the weather*, and the things that are being compared are now logically comparable.

Error 2) Steven King is more prolific than any novelists in his era.

You cannot compare something with a group that includes that thing. It should be corrected as follows.

Corr. 2) Steven King is more prolific than any other novelist in his era.

You have to add *other* in this kind of comparison. Furthermore, you normally use a singular noun *novelist* instead of *novelists*. You can also use *(all) the other novelists* after *than*.

> *Error 3) The friends of hers who came here yesterday are more polite than them.*

For logical comparison, you have to match the case of the pronoun, too.

> *Corr. 3) The friends of hers who came here yesterday are more polite than they (are).*

The *friends of hers*, which is used as the subject, must be compared with *they*, the subjective case, not *them*, the objective case.

☞ **Note**: You don't have to worry too much about these somewhat meticulous rules in a casual speech or writing, but in a formal speech or writing, you have to avoid these errors for effective and unambiguous rendition of your intended message.

☞ **Note**: This logical comparison rules apply to all types of comparisons in the following subsections. **So pay attention and verify that the things that are being compared in all the following examples are logically comparable.**

Q: Correct the following sentence.

The judges decided that the rocker was more prettier than any singer in that competition, but other contestants thought that the way she sang was worser than an ordinary person.

10.2 Modifying Comparatives and Superlatives

10.2.1 Modifying Comparatives

> *Ex 1)   The University of Chicago Economics PhD Program is way more prestigious than any other Economics PhD Program.*

There are adverbs used to indicate the degree by which things under comparison differ. The following words can modify comparatives in a decreasing extent of difference: *way, far, whole lot, a lot, much, a good deal, significantly, considerably, noticeably, somewhat, a little, a little bit, slightly, hardly, scarcely,* etc.

10.2.2 Modifying Superlatives

> *Ex 1)*   *The Johns Hopkins Hospital is <u>by far</u> <u>the</u> <u>most</u> eminent*
>   *hospital in the world.*

The following words can modify superlatives: *by far, quite, absolutely, undoubtedly, practically,* etc.

> *Ex 1)*   *The Harvard University is <u>the</u> <u>very</u> <u>best</u> <u>and</u> <u>oldest</u> <u>college</u> that*
>   *was founded in the U.S.A.*

Unlike other adverbs, you have to put the definite article *the* **in front of** the adverb *very* to modify superlatives.

10.3 Similarity

10.3.1 *The Same* and *The Same* As

> *Ex 1)*   *These shoes and those shoes are <u>the same</u> (shoes).*

> *Ex 2)*   *All of them are <u>the same</u>.*

> *Ex 3)*   *This house is almost <u>the same</u> <u>as</u> that house.*

> *Ex 4)*   *This is <u>the same</u> <u>house</u> <u>as</u> that.*

You use *the same* to indicate exact likeness. By attaching an adverb such as *almost* and *approximately*, you can make it not so exactly alike.

> *Ex 5)*   *This house is <u>the same</u> <u>price</u> <u>as</u> that house.*

A quality noun *price* is used to compare a specific quality of the two objects being compared. **Quality nouns** such as *age, color, depth, height, length, price, size, style, volume, weight, width*, etc. can be used in this structure.

☞ *Note*: Avoid **illogical comparison** errors for this structure, too.

> *Error 1)* <u>The pineapples of China</u> are almost the same as <u>India</u>.

> *Corr. 1)* <u>The pineapples of China</u> are almost the same as <u>those of India</u>.

10.3.2 *Alike* and *Like*

> *Ex 1)*   These shoes and those shoes are <u>alike</u>.

> *Ex 2)*   All of them are <u>alike</u>.

> *Ex 3)*   This house is almost <u>like</u> that house.

You use *alike* and *like* to indicate close similarity or likeness. *Alike* is a **predicate adjective** (refer to Predicate Adjective (5.7)) and thus can be used only as a subjective or objective complement (i.e., *alike* cannot be placed before a noun to modify it). *Like* is a preposition when used in this way.

☞ *Note*: Avoid **illogical comparison** errors for this structure.

> *Error 1)* <u>Like the shoes</u> made by Adidas, <u>Nike</u> makes use of the new technology.

> *Corr. 1)* <u>Like the shoes</u> made by Adidas, <u>those</u> made by Nike use the new technology.

10.3.3 *Similar* and *Similar To*

> *Ex 1)*   These shoes and those shoes are <u>similar</u>.

> *Ex 2)*   All of them are <u>similar</u>.

> *Ex 3)*   This house is <u>similar to</u> that house.

You use *similar* and *similar to* to show general similarity

☞ *Note*: Avoid **illogical comparison** errors for this structure.

> *Q: Correct the following sentence.*
>
> The choreography done by those hip-hop dancers was, unlike the ballet dancers, almost the same as break dancers.

10.4 As ~ As ~

10.4.1 Similarity

> *Ex 1)*   <u>This gigantic tree</u> is <u>as</u> <u>old</u> <u>as</u> <u>this castle</u>.

To compare two things that are similar in a specific quality, you can use [as] + [adjective] + [as] + [a noun to which the noun before it is compared].

Ex 2) *This LCD TV is as expensive an electronic system in the house as this ultramodern computer.*

Ex 3) *That actress is very gorgeous; surprisingly enough, the reporters found her mother as gorgeous (as her).*

As Ex 3 shows, you can omit the last as phrase (in Ex 3, *as her*) when it is obvious.

Ex 4) *The credibility of my mentor is as high as that of your mentor.*

Notice that logical comparison was made in Ex 4.

10.4.2 Magnitude of Difference

Ex 1) *My boss's asset is five times as much as mine.*

Ex 2) *My brother has three times as many children as I.*

Ex 3) *Her mother is twice as old as she.*

you want to specify the magnitude of difference, you can use multiple numbers such as *one third, half, twice, three times, four times*, etc. in front of *as ~ as ~* (using *twice/three times more than ~* is wrong). Notice again that the comparisons are logically made and that subjective pronouns are used after the second *as* because they are compared with the subjects of the sentences.

☞ *Note*: *As many as* and *as much as* can be used as adverbial phrases modifying a specific number, and they mean *nearly*. However, *as much as* can be used in this way only in front of specific numbers that refer to an amount (for example, distance, height, weight, amount of money, etc.).

Ex 4) *As many as five thousand physicists and chemists showed up in the convention.*

Ex 5) *We have to have as much as five billion dollars for the reconstruction project.*

10.4.3 Expressing Semi-Superlatives Using As~ As~

> Ex 1) *The weather in San Francisco is as good as that in any other city in the world.*

Notice a singular noun is used after *any other.*

> Ex 2) *No (other) city is as luxurious and dazzling as New York.*

> *Q: Correct the following sentence.*
>
> *The plot of the mini-series was as impeccably executed as any program.*

10.5 General Difference/Contrast

10.5.1 Differ From/Different From

> Ex 1) *Graduate courses differ from undergraduate courses.*

> Ex 2) *The courses in professional schools are very different from those in undergraduate schools.*

Formal English requires you to use *from* rather than *than* with *differ* or *different.* In certain idiomatic expressions such as "*I beg to differ with you,*" you use *with* instead of *from.*

10.5.2 Opposite/The Opposite/Contrast With

> Ex 1) *This couple and that couple are opposite in their lifestyles.*

> Ex 2) *The lifestyle of this couple is the opposite of that of that couple.*

> Ex 2) *These methods contrast with those approaches. The teacher contrasted these methods with those approaches.*

We have seen other ways to express contrast in the conjunction chapter (section 8.2)

10.6 Double Comparatives.

> *Ex 1)* _The more you study_ with Optimal English series, _the more efficient your English will be._
>
> ≈ *If you study with Optimal English series more, your English will be more efficient.*

The basic structure of double comparatives is [The] + [the comparative of an adjective or an adverb] + [Subject] + [Verb], [the] + [the comparative of an adjective or an adverb] + [Subject] + [Verb]

There are other examples in The for Other Special Cases (5.2.3.4).

> **Q: Correct the following sentence.**
>
> *The greater your English skills become, more different you are likely to become than your peers.*

10.7 Chapter Exam on Comparisons

Find all grammar errors and correct them most efficiently. The following sentences may contain one, multiple, or no error(s).

1) This Korean dish is a most unique one because it tastes different than any dish.

2) His wealth is ten times more than my wealth, but his reputation is badder than me.

3) There are less people in the mall because alike malls have appeared in that city where as much as two million people live.

4) Among the three superintendents, Mr. Lucas is the more intellectual person, but the other two superintendents keep on insisting that their intelligence is as well as Mr. Lucas.

5) The cousins of the heroine loved her son more than she after he saved their village from various monsters' attacks which were like the anthropophagous barbarians, but she did not come to help them.

"Choose my instruction instead of silver, knowledge rather than choice gold,
for wisdom is more precious than rubies, and nothing you desire
can compare with her."
- Proverbs 8:10-11

"I don't think much of a man who is not wiser today than he was yesterday."
- Abraham Lincoln

"What is a college? An institute of learning. What is a business?
An institute of learning. Life itself is an institute of learning."
- Thomas Edison

"Who so neglects learning in his youth loses
the past and is dead for the future."
- Euripides

"There are two kinds of men: one who has the learning attitude and
the other without it. There are two kinds of the former:
one who seeks to learn optimally and the other who doesn't."
- Paul S. Lee

OPTIMAL ENGLISH GRAMMAR

Part 2

STYLE

11 Agreement

Agreement is a very important concept in all language, especially in English. Parts of a sentence must agree with one another for consistency. There are several kinds of agreement: subject-verb agreement, noun-pronoun agreement, tense agreement, noun-appositive agreement, etc.

11.1 Subject-Verb Agreement

Ex 1) *The chief of staff, along with tens of the sagacious young men, does a great job for the President.*

You always have to make sure that the verb (in Ex 1, *does*) agrees with the true subject of the clause (in Ex 1, *The chief of staff*). Be careful not to mistake *men* as the subject of the verb *does*. The phrase *along with tens of the sagacious young men* is called **a parenthetical phrase** (usually separated by commas) that does not affect the form of the verb and simply modifies the noun before it.

Ex 2) *The quality of all the exported products is exceptionally commendable.*

Again, the subject of the sentence is *The quality*, not *products;* thus, the verb has to be *is* not *are*. The modifying phrase, *of all the exported products*, is also a parenthetical phrase that does not affect the verb. These modifying parenthetical expressions are adjectival phrases and clauses (refer to Adjectival Phrases and Clauses (5.10)).

☞ *Note*: You have to use a plural verb in the relative pronoun clause when *one of the* ~ is the antecedent; on the other hand, you have to use a singular verb in the relative pronoun clause when *the only one of* ~ is the antecedent.

Ex 3) *I am one of the apostates who are from the left. You are the only one of the apostates who is from the right.*

☞ *Note*: Another very important and tricky case of subject-verb agreement appears in **inverted** sentences. Refer to Inversion (6.6)

☞ *Note*: Most of the basic subject-verb agreement was already covered in sections on noun, pronoun, and conjunction (especially correlative conjunctions). You have to know whether the noun or compound noun should be treated as singular or as plural (refer to 3.6).

11.2 Noun-Appositive Agreement

Error 1) The <u>professors</u> of the University of Chicago Department of Economics, the most distinguished <u>scholar</u> in the field, strive to pioneer new methods of combining Economics theory and numerical simulation.

Here, the phrase between commas is called **the appositive** of the noun that it refers to. The appositive and the noun that it refers to must agree in number and gender; thus, *scholar* which refers to *professors* (which is plural) must be *scholars*.

11.3 Noun-Pronoun / Pronoun-Pronoun / Noun-Noun Agreement

Error 1) When the <u>rascals</u> tried to tease the substitute teacher who looked inexperienced, she strictly warned <u>him</u> to focus on the class work.

Whenever a pronoun refers to a noun either within the same clause or across clauses, it has to agree with the noun in number and gender; thus, the pronoun *him* referring to *rascals* should be corrected as *them*.

☞ **_Note_**: In formal writing, you have to choose carefully which **relative pronoun** to use for a certain kind of antecedent. Refer to Relative Pronouns (section 4.10).

Error 2) When <u>one</u> doesn't have a legitimate visa to the U.S.A., <u>you</u> will be required to leave the country.

Because an indefinite pronoun *one* was used before, the subject of the main clause *you* should be changed to *one*.

☞ **_Note_**: You have to be careful that when you use a definite pronoun, the pronoun must have an unambiguous antecedent. In formal writing, **pronoun ambiguity** is also a common error that you must avoid.

Error 3) <u>His mother</u> told <u>his aunt</u> that <u>she</u> had to be more careful about the assignments.

Corr 3) <u>His mother</u> told <u>his aunt</u> that <u>his aunt</u> (or his mother) had to be more careful about the assignments.

☞ **_Note_**: You have to be careful that when a person/thing or persons/things become somebody/something or some people/some things, these nouns must be consistent in number.

> *Error 4)* <u>*My brothers* *became*</u> <u>*a doctor.*</u> <u>*Beauty*</u> <u>*and*</u> <u>*intelligence*</u> <u>*are*</u> <u>*the*</u> <u>*criterion.*</u>

> *Corr 4)* <u>*My brothers*</u> <u>*became*</u> <u>*doctors.*</u> <u>*Beauty*</u> <u>*and*</u> <u>*intelligence*</u> <u>*are*</u> <u>*the*</u> <u>*criteria.*</u>

11.4 Tense Agreement

Refer to Tense (2.2). Furthermore, refer to Participial Phrase (2.4.4) on using [*Having*] + [Past Participle] in participial phrases (especially Ex 4).

11.5 Chapter Exam on Agreement

Find all grammar errors and correct them most efficiently. The following sentences may contain one, multiple, or no error(s).

1) Only when the young student who attends a very expensive private school receive a high score on the SAT is his father, a prominent lawyer who works at one of the most prestigious law firms, and his mother, a respected doctor, likely to allow her son to get a car.

2) When the lady saw the majestic view, she had felt a great renewing of her mind.

3) By the time my sons and daughters reach the age of 40, all of them will become a missionary.

4) By the time the girl and her grandmother finished that project which required a substantial amount of time, she wrote at least 9 creative papers.

5) The special situations where my brazen cousin feels embarrassed is hard to observe.

12   Redundancy

Redundancy in style means an unnecessary repetition of words with the same meaning, or more broadly, using more words than necessary. Unless you need to repeat an idea intentionally for emphasis, you should avoid redundant expressions.

12.1 Repetition of words with the same meaning

Error 1) Her midnight visit was an unexpected surprise.

Surprise means *unexpected thing or event*, so you had better not repeat *unexpected*. Change *an unexpected surprise* to *a surprise*.

Error 2) Can you repeat that statement again?

Repeat means *say or do again*, so you had better not attach *again* after *repeat*.

Here are some of the numerous common redundancy-related expressions (the underlined part is often redundant):

- **Advance:** *advance forward, advance planning, advance preview, advance reservations, advance warning, plan in advance, warn in advance*, etc.

- **Again:** *recur again, redo again, retry again, repeat again, reproduce again*, etc.

- **Back:** *extradite back, refer back to, reflect back, regress back, reply back, retreat back, retrospect back, revert back*, etc.

- **Completely:** *completely annihilate, completely complete, completely eradicate, completely perfect*, etc.

- **Final:** *final conclusion, final end, final outcome, final ultimatum, final finale*, etc.

- **New:** *new beginning, new innovation, new invention, new recruit, new news, new novice*, etc.

- **Old:** *old adage, old ancient, old cliché, old proverb*, etc.

- **Past:** *past experience, past history, past memories, past records*, etc.

- **Together:** *assemble <u>together</u>, attach <u>together</u>, collaborate <u>together</u>, combine <u>together</u>, connect <u>together</u>, fuse <u>together</u>, gather <u>together</u>, integrate <u>together</u>, join <u>together</u>, meet <u>together</u>, merge <u>together</u>, share <u>together</u>, splice <u>together</u>,* etc.

- **Others:** *sufficient enough* (only one of them should be used), *nearly almost* (only one of them should be used), *ascend <u>up</u>, descend <u>down</u>, circulate <u>around</u>, pursue <u>after</u>, follow <u>after</u>, lag <u>behind</u>, may/might <u>possibly</u>, remain <u>to go</u>,* etc.

Also refer to Redundant Prepositions (7.6).

Some of these expressions are often used and may, in some context, add some additional meaning or emphasis, but **others are considered flagrant (*repeat again, retry again, refer back, new innovation, final ultimatum, sufficient enough, nearly almost*, etc.) and wrong, not just inefficient, in formal writing.**

12.2 Modifying Absolute Adjectives/Adverbs

Error 1) This English grammar book is <u>very</u> <u>optimal</u> for Korean students as well as for other students of various national origins.

As we have studied in Absolute Adjectives and Adverbs (section 10.1.5), there are adjectives or adverbs (such as *absolute, complete, entire, fatal, final, ideal, impossible, indispensable, inevitable, optimal, supreme, ultimate, universal, unique,* etc.) that cannot be modified in certain ways (as in Error 1) or made into comparatives or superlatives simply because they represent some absolute or incomparable quality. So, in formal writing, you should avoid using these absolute adjectives or adverbs with such adverbs as *very, most, more*, etc.

12.3 Double Negatives

Error 1) I <u>cannot</u> <u>hardly</u> wait for you to return to me.

You should avoid using negative words such as *no, not, never, few, little, hardly, rarely, scarcely, seldom, none, nobody, nothing*, etc. together in the same clause. So for Error 1, you should use either *can hardly* or *cannot*, but not *cannot hardly* because it is a double negative.

Error 2) The convict <u>didn't</u> say <u>nothing</u>.

Corr 2) The convict <u>said nothing</u>. The convict <u>didn't</u> say <u>anything</u>.

12.4 Lengthier Phrases

Error 1) My protégé followed my edification in a perfect manner.

Economy of language tells us to use shorter expressions unless they change the intended meaning of the sentence. Using *perfectly* is better than using a lengthy expression *in a perfect manner.*

Error 2) The grandmaster disciplined his students in a way that is very strict.

Corr 2) The grandmaster disciplined his students very strictly.

12.5 Chapter Exam on Redundancy

Find all grammar errors and correct them most efficiently. The following sentences may contain one, multiple, or no error(s).

1) When I couldn't understand the mechanism behind the new innovation, the developer repeated it again for me.

2) This house has a most unique structure and is more optimal than any other house.

3) The new hybrid car will not, unless its price decreases, hardly sell to a sufficiently enough large number of consumers.

4) "This is the final ultimatum!" shouted the general.

5) The manager did not refer back to nothing special.

13 Parallelism and logical Comparison

Error 1) <u>*Studying with the right material*</u>, <u>*learning from an experienced teacher,*</u> *and* <u>*to review properly what you learned*</u> *are more important factors for success in mastering English than* <u>*by only speaking with native Americans.*</u>

Parallelism and illogical comparison, which could be considered a violation of parallelism, are also very important concepts in style. These concepts are already covered in Parallelism (section 8.4) and Illogical Comparison (section 10.1.6). In summary, parallelism means listing ideas in the same grammatical structure or style, and logical comparison means comparing ideas in the same category. Thus, Error 1 must have all gerund phrases in the compound subject as well as in the compared place (after *than*) to satisfy parallelism and logical comparison.

Corr 1) <u>*Studying with the right material*</u>, <u>*learning from an experienced teacher,*</u> *and* <u>*reviewing properly what you learned*</u> *are more important factors for success in mastering English than* <u>*only speaking with native Americans.*</u>

If you want some exercise problems on parallelism and logical comparison, review chapter exams on conjunctions and comparisons (chapters 8 and 10).

14 Modifier Problems

Modifiers must be as close to the word they modify as structurally permissible; otherwise, there could result in some ambiguity.

14.1 Unclear Position of Modifiers

Error 1) <u>Only</u> <u>he</u> *can sleep on that soft bed, so she has to clean it right now.*

It seems as if there is nothing wrong with this sentence grammatically; however, when you analyze its context, this sentence doesn't make much sense. "Her having to clean the bed because he is the only person who can sleep on it" does not flow logically. The following corrected sentence makes much more sense.

Corr 1) *He can sleep* <u>only</u> <u>on that soft bed,</u> *so she has to clean it right now.*

So, as was discussed in Order of Adverbs (section 6.3), the general rule for placing a modifier is that the modifier should be as close to the word it modifies as possible. For a simple adverb, you usually place it right in front of the word it modifies (verb, adjective, adverb, or whole sentence). For a simple adjective, you put it in front of the noun it modifies, and for an adjectival phrase or clause, you put it right after the noun it modifies (refer to section 5.10).

Error 2) *The colonel who* <u>shouted</u> *at his troop* <u>energetically</u> <u>ran</u> *toward the enemy.*

Here, the adverb *energetically* can be considered to modify the verb *shouted* or the verb *ran*. This type of ambiguous modifier is called a **squinting modifier.** A squinting modifier basically can modify either a preceding or following word and makes the sentence very unclear.

Corr 2A) *The colonel who* <u>energetically</u> *shouted at his troop ran toward the enemy.* (*energetically* modifies *shouted*)

Corr 2B) *The colonel who shouted at his troop ran* <u>energetically</u> *toward the enemy.* (*energetically* modifies *ran*)

14.2 Dangling Modifiers

Dangling modifier problem is a common mistake a lot of people make. Refer to Dangling Participial/Gerund/Infinitive Phrases (Section 2.4.5).

☞ **_Note_**: Avoid also dangling appositives. An appositive must be the same entity as the noun it modifies; otherwise, it is a dangling phrase, too.

> _Error 1) Sonata and Elantra, the modern engines made by Hyundai, are the results of millions of hours of research._

Sonata and Elantra are not engines but cars. You may correct the sentence in two ways depending on your intended meaning.

> _Corr 1A) Sonata and Elantra, the cars with the modern engines made by Hyundai, are the results of millions of hours of research._

> _Corr 1B) The engines of Sonata and Elantra, the modern engines made by Hyundai, are the results of millions of hours of research._

15   Diction (Word Choice)

Diction errors occur when you choose the wrong word among tricky or similar words.

15.1 Prepositional Idioms

Error 1) The duchess was preoccupied to her daughter's urgent matrimony.

Preoccupied to is incorrect; *preoccupied with* should be used instead.

Refer to Preposition-Related Diction (Section 7.4). To be free from errors of this kind, you will have to master idioms.

15.2 Parts of Speech

Error 1) This recipe requires very special prepared condiments.

In context, *special* above modifies adjective *prepared*, so you have to use the adverb *specially*.

Using parts of speech in the right place of the sentence was basically one of the most important themes in Part 2 (Parts of Speech) and in this book. You simply have to improve your vocabulary with strong knowledge of the words' parts of speech. Pay special attention to the diction-related sections in each of the previous (chapters 2 through 10) chapters.

15.3 Intransitive Verbs vs Transitive Verbs

One of the common diction-related errors is made when you use transitive verbs and intransitive verbs incorrectly. As was discussed in The Five Basic Patterns (Chapter 1), intransitive verbs do not have an object whereas transitive verbs need an object. Here are some of the most confusing verb pairs of this type:

- *Lie-lay-lain* vs *lay-laid-laid:*

  Ex 1)   Before my aunt lay on her bed, she had laid all her burdens under God.

☞ __*Note*__: These two verbs are especially confusing since the past form of the intransitive verb *lie* is *lay*, which happens to be the same as the transitive verb *lay*. To determine which verb is the correct one to use, you have to check whether the verb has an object and which tense should be used.

- **Rise-rose-risen** vs **Raise-raised-raised:**

  Ex 2)   *When the sun <u>rises</u> from the east, make sure you <u>raise</u> <u>our glorious flag.</u>*

- **Sit-sat-sat** vs **Set-set-set:**

  Ex 3)   *The moment the professor emeritus <u>sat</u> down, the assistant professor <u>set</u> <u>the lectern</u> for him.*

15.4 Other Confusing Words

There are other often-confused words. Here are some of the examples:

- **Former** and **Latter** vs **First** and **Last**: Use *the former* to refer to the first item in a series of two and *the latter* to refer to the second item. When talking about three or more items, use *the first, the second, the last,* etc.

  Ex 1)   *The association had to elect <u>the president</u> and <u>the treasurer</u>; <u>the former</u> has to be at least 40 years old, and <u>the latter</u>, at least 35.*

- **Hanged** vs **Hung**: *Hanged* and *hung* are both the past participle of *hang*. *Hanged* means *executed on a gallows* and *hung* means *suspended*.

  Ex 2)   *The rebel was eventually <u>hanged</u> in the public square, and his body was <u>hung</u> on the gallows.*

- **The Reason That:** In a very formal setting, *The Reason* should be followed by *that*, and neither by *because* nor by *why* even though in many formal settings, the *reason why* is often used.

  Error 1) <u>The reason why</u> he is the winner is obvious. <u>The reason</u> he won that award is <u>because</u> he contributed most to the success of the project.

  Corr 1) <u>The reason that</u> he is the winner is obvious. <u>The reason</u> he won that award is <u>that</u> he contributed most to the success of the project.

= He won that award <u>because</u> he contributed most to the success of the project.

- **Likely to** vs **Liable to:** *Liable to* is used only with verbs that show bad results such as *sink, fail, flounder, collapse*, etc. *Likely to* can be used with any verb.

- **Others:** *accept* vs *except, adapt* vs *adept, affect* vs *effect, all ready* vs *already, all together* vs *altogether, allude* vs *elude, credible* vs *credulous, compliment* vs *complement, complacent* vs *complaisant, discrete* vs *discreet, elicit* vs *illicit, imply* vs *infer, indecisive* vs *indefinite, perspective* vs *prospective, phase* vs *faze, principal* vs *principle*, etc.

  Understand the exact definitions of these words that sound very similar or the same.

☞ <u>Note</u>: You have to be extra careful about these so-called **homophones** (the words that sound the same) in identifying diction errors.

15.5 Chapter Exam on Diction

Find all grammar errors and correct them most efficiently. The following sentences may contain one, multiple, or no error(s).

1) The accusations lay out in the media were preposterous and increasing unbearable.

2) The principle reason why North Korea still suffers under a dictator is because its people are not sufficiently informed about how different other people in the world live.

3) My sly cousin is liable to inherit a great amount of wealth from his grandfather, who is, despite having great business acumen, credible.

4) Discreet mathematics compliments continuous mathematics.

5) The riverside smelled quite greatly from the affect of the revitalizing spring rain, and it was capable to refresh my mind.

16 Comprehensive Exam on *Optimal English Grammar*

Find all grammar errors and correct them most efficiently. The following sentences may contain one, multiple, or no error(s).

1) Every one of the successful people are characterized as well-organized and well-prepared for the matters they want accomplishing; the lives of the majority of the prominent lawyers, CEOs, and doctors' jobs demonstrate that they are a master of planning ahead for important events or projects.

2) While I cannot impugn the argument that too many inflexible planning and execution may interfere with creativity that might arise at an unexpected moment, if properly applied, I can unambiguously see that great planning in fact can foster creativity.

3) Many of the great literary works, especially novelists and biographers, are creations from great planning and background research, to make a creative and well-written story, a period of intense cerebration and plotting must be applied by an author so that the story becomes novel and creative, full of both surprises and of interesting events.

4) Without great planning, authors are likely to not only produce incoherent but also hackneyed and anticlimactic storyline that will leave the readers feeling exasperatedly about them wasting precious time.

5) Only by detailed planning author can minimize the unnecessary time cost of having to revise the entire book and the risk of publishing a disappointed book, thereby damaging their reputation.

6) It is imperative that the director, that is the planner, produces a memorable concert, a unforgettable musical as well as producing a spectacular show, fraught with creative programs and events.

7) The blockbuster concerts or musicals that enjoy the ongoing utmost popularity is a product of extensive and impeccable planning and coordinating where there is no room for error; not only the producers but also the director try hardly to meet the plan.

8) The planning team does their best to incorporate creativity and innovations into the project; but, when the plan is finalized, all participants stick to the plan.

9) By meeting the expected course of action, the audience can find that the artists can maximally show the intended creativity and quality; the viewers would have shown disappointment if they would not have found it.

10) There are, of course, some instances when spontaneous deviations from the plan must be allowed to produce the optimal result; for example, many jazz concerts where the musicians must be allowed to improvise according to the mood of the ambience and avoiding following mechanically premeditated actions.

11) Yet, even for this kind of occasion, for maximizing the intended result, great planning must be capable to take into account all contingency plans, therefore, I strongly believe that planning, doing properly and thoroughly by taking all possibilities into account, do not hardly interfere with creativity.

12) Overall, planning can be beneficial: An usual planner might not have the ability of concocting and balancing planning and creativity, a honorable planner, that is preoccupied by making the perfect amalgamation, may use them as if they are one and produce more unique and optimal result in which the audience fall in love.

Appendix 2: Answers for Chapter Exams

CHAPTER EXAM ON BASICS

Indicate to which basic pattern the following sentences belong and the words that are the essential components of the basic pattern and indicate what they are (i.e., subject, verb, direct object, indirect object, subjective complement, objective complement). Also put a bracket around the clauses in the sentence and indicate what they are (whether independent or subordinate clause).

1. {When she came to the U.S.A.}, {she looked unbelievably vivacious according to what most of the people who knew her said.}

   Basic Pattern 2: "looked" is an incomplete intransitive or a linking verb in this sentence.

2. {If I saw you again}, {I would have you come and live with me for the rest of your life in my stunningly fabulous house custom-made for you.}

   Basic Pattern 5: "have" is an incomplete transitive verb in this sentence.

3. {I know {that I will never be thirsty anymore} because of the ever-flowing fountain of your love.}

   Basic Pattern 3: "know" is a complete transitive verb in this sentence.

4. {Could you please bring me that tasty fruit {that you picked in the orchard?}}

   Basic Pattern 4: "bring" is a "give" verb in this sentence.

5. {In the middle of the Korean War {when my whole family had to move all the way to Pusan {where there was nobody {who was nice enough to help us}}}, our parents stood alone in that unfamiliar territory.}

   Basic Pattern 1: "stood" is a complete intransitive verb in this sentence.

Find all grammar errors and correct them most efficiently (with minimal change). The following sentences may contain one, multiple, or no error(s).

6. All dishes in this restaurant tasted unbelievably ~~badly~~bad and everybody who ate there felt very ~~uncomfortably~~uncomfortable.

CHAPTER EXAM ON VERBS

Find all grammar errors and correct them most efficiently. The following sentences may contain one, multiple, or no error(s).

1) Socrates <u>was</u> born to a mason father and a midwife mother in 469 when the Sophists, the philosophers who enjoyed ~~to argue~~arguing with one another, ~~was~~were dominant.

2) Plato would not ~~be~~ have been able to establish Academia, the center of education in that era, if Socrates ~~would~~ had not ~~have~~ influenced him, ; however, Plato created his own unique philosophy.

3) The ambition of the emperor ~~had~~ ended when he became seriously ill, so he requested that every child of his attend~~ed~~ his presumably last birthday party.

4) The queen got her nephew <u>to</u> take her throne~~, ;~~ after hesitating for a while, he eventually accepted.

5) The admiral whose reputation is well-known in many countries ~~say~~ <u>says</u> that he will <u>have</u> construct~~ed~~ 100 ships by the time the enemy invades our sea, yet the king does not believe what ~~is he~~he is saying, fearing that he may fail ~~accomplishing~~ to accomplish that project.

6) No sooner <u>had</u> the car ~~was~~ <u>been</u> fixed ~~when~~ <u>than</u> my daughter drove it away.

7) Renowned for his brilliant expressions, ~~people~~ <u>the journalist was</u> call<u>ed</u> ~~the journalist~~ "the word whiz," and his creative use of words made him ~~to~~ receive the prestigious journalist award.

8) When the imperial soldiers came back from the war, the Indian chief clearly remember<u>ed</u> ~~them~~ <u>their</u> demolishing his land.

9) The physicist must <u>have</u> be<u>en</u> absorbed ~~with~~ <u>in</u> his research when his fiancée came to see him: He ~~did~~ <u>had</u> not see<u>n</u> her for almost 3 years.

10) Unlike his predecessor, the new president was accustomed to speak<u>ing</u> in English while meeting with other CEOs; and also skilled in effective communication, ~~his leadership~~he had ~~was~~ outstanding <u>leadership</u>.

CHAPTER EXAM ON NOUNS

Find all grammar errors and correct them most efficiently. The following sentences may contain one, multiple, or no error(s).

1) The teacher is nicknamed "the walking dictionary" because he has memorized <u>an</u> entire dictionary that contains 60,000 word<u>s</u>.

2) "The boisterous crowd of millions of indignant people ~~are~~ <u>is</u> marching toward the state capitol, but five miles of walking ~~are~~ <u>is</u> not easy for most of them," reported the veteran reporter about one of the emerging ~~phenomenons~~<u>phenomena</u>.

3) Billiards ~~are~~ <u>is</u> one of the best sports that gentlemen can enjoy because simple physics ~~are~~ <u>is</u> all it requires.

4) The friend and patron ~~were~~ <u>was</u> the one I chose as the godfather for my son for the ~~criterions~~ <u>criteria</u> I applied are integrity and trustworthiness.

5) When I heard those five loud ~~thunders~~<u>claps of thunder</u>, I began to shudder involuntarily because of the nightmarish ~~poetries~~ <u>poems</u> I had read when the only pair of eyeglasses I had ~~were~~ <u>was</u> broken.

CHAPTER EXAM ON PRONOUNS

Find all grammar errors and correct them most efficiently. The following sentences may contain one, multiple, or no error(s).

1) The four defendants were ~~us~~<u>we</u>, and the justice ordered every one of ~~we~~ <u>us</u> defendants not to talk to ~~each other~~<u>one another</u> during the hearing.

2) Because only the Constitution can mediate between the unbridled authoritarian government and ~~we~~<u>us</u>, our senators objected to ~~him~~ <u>his</u> speaking against the U.S. Constitution and said that he should be ashamed of him<u>self</u> for doing ~~them~~ <u>it</u>.

3) The athlete is the one ~~that~~ <u>who</u> received the gold medal and made a sensation ~~where~~ <u>in which</u> our countrymen became obsessed with ~~them~~ following in his footsteps.

4)   At the end of the day, the computer, ~~that~~ <u>which</u> was developed most recently, will dominate ~~their~~ <u>its</u> market.

5)   God will show his mercy to ~~whomever~~ <u>whoever</u> will obey His commandments, and His servants in that church, ~~whom~~ <u>who</u> I believe ~~has~~ <u>have</u> great faith, will be abundantly rewarded.

CHAPTER EXAM ON ADJECTIVES

Find all grammar errors and correct them most efficiently. The following sentences may contain one, multiple, or no error(s).

1)   The Arabian was so ~~a~~ skilled <u>an</u> artisan that he was capable ~~to~~ <u>of</u> ~~produce~~ <u>producing</u> thousand-pound~~s~~ metalwares.

2)   ~~An~~ <u>A</u> usual thing that he exhibited was such <u>a</u> normal ~~a~~ habit that any ~~asleep~~ <u>sleeping</u> child can show.

3)   The ~~m~~<u>M</u>usic of Hawaii is warm and blissful, but ~~less~~ <u>fewer</u> full-time Hawaiian musicians live there ~~due to~~<u>because of</u> the low pay they receive in that island.

4)   You have to make him sit on <u>a</u> chair and calm down; otherwise, he, ashamed ~~for~~ <u>of</u> his wrongdoing, may do things that will hurt <u>his</u> body.

5)   A great number of beautiful swan~~s~~ ~~is~~ <u>are</u> swimming on the lake; however, that ugly bird is also a kind of ~~a~~ swan and is not ~~such~~ <u>very</u> different ~~with~~ <u>from</u> the other kind.

CHAPTER EXAM ON ADVERBS

Find all grammar errors and correct them most efficiently. The following sentences may contain one, multiple, or no error(s).

1)   The president hates people who are not on time; ~~furthermore~~<u>nevertheless</u>, his chief spokesperson came to the meeting late~~ly~~.

2)   The trumpeter has <u>never</u> played ~~never~~ the trombone and is very unskilled with it; yet, not until we find a professional trombonist ~~he will~~<u>will he</u> stop playing it.

3) Between a huge dragon and a colossal giant ~~does~~ stand a vulnerable little girl who is less than four feet tall and a shabby dog ~~stand~~.

4) My essays are marked by brevity, and so ~~do~~ are my poems; only when I become an inefficient person ~~I will~~will I start writing lengthier essays and poems.

5) Wonderful ~~is~~ are the woman who gave birth to the child and the man who gladly took the child as his own; not many people will ~~hardly~~ become ungrateful for their sacrifice.

CHAPTER EXAM ON PREPOSITIONS

Find all grammar errors and correct them most efficiently. The following sentences may contain one, multiple, or no error(s).

1) My assistant had lived ~~on~~ at 1200 Jimmy Carter Boulevard for 35 years; his preoccupation ~~in~~ with living there differs ~~with~~ from my obsession ~~for~~ with living ~~at~~ in Seoul.

2) The parents were looking forward to ~~participate~~ participating ~~on~~ in the Christmas event, to be held ~~in~~ at 5:00 p.m. ~~at~~ in Atlanta, GA.

3) The evening in which his girlfriend agreed ~~with~~ to his offer was ~~in~~ on the same day as the morning ~~on~~ in which her ex-boyfriend fell off ~~of~~ a long ladder and broke his legs.

4) Besides the biologist's great I.Q., her strong willpower also contributed ~~on~~ to her winning the award ~~between~~ among the three candidates.

5) The colonel said that ~~for winning~~to win a battle, the most important thing is for the soldiers to have the desire ~~of~~ for victory and the commitment ~~on~~ to patriotism because they can only resort ~~on~~ to one another.

CHAPTER EXAM ON CONJUNCTIONS

Find all grammar errors and correct them most efficiently. The following sentences may contain one, multiple, or no error(s).

1) Both the fact that he was a former felon and <u>that</u> his wife~~'s having been~~<u>was</u> a famous swindler makes it difficult for the couple to live either in that high-class subdivision or <u>in</u> the other opulent neighborhood.

2) The pilots can get their training <u>not only</u> in ~~not only~~ the airfield but also in the simulation room in order ~~that~~ <u>to</u> acquire their certificates.

3) Just as the emperor was hailed in the whole empire, ~~as~~ so too <u>was</u> the governor ~~did~~ in his province.

4) Neither the democrats who occupied more than 60 percent of the House <u>n</u>or the Speaker of the House who had the President on his side ~~were~~ <u>was</u> able to satisfy the citizens of the United States.

5) The people of Korea, who are famous for their efficiency, the people of Japan, who are well-known for their service, <u>and</u> the people of China, who are recognized for their productivity, as well as ~~Americans~~<u>the people of America</u>, who are known widely ~~to be creative~~<u>for their creativity</u>, are competing for dominance in the world's export market.

CHAPTER EXAM ON COMPARISONS

Find all grammar errors and correct them most efficiently. The following sentences may contain one, multiple, or no error(s).

1) This Korean dish is a ~~most~~ unique one because it tastes different ~~than~~ <u>from</u> any <u>other</u> dish.

2) His wealth is ten times ~~more than~~<u>as much as</u> my wealth, but his reputation is ~~badder~~ <u>worse</u> than ~~me~~<u>mine</u>.

3) There are ~~less~~ <u>fewer</u> people in the mall because ~~alike~~ <u>similar</u> malls have appeared in that city where as ~~much~~ <u>many</u> as two million people live.

4) Among the three superintendents, Mr. Lucas is the ~~more~~ <u>most</u> intellectual person, but the other two superintendents keep on insisting that their intelligence is as ~~well~~ <u>good</u> as <u>that of</u> Mr. Lucas.

5) The cousins of the heroin loved her son more than ~~she~~ <u>her</u> after he saved their village from various monsters' attacks which were like <u>those of</u> the anthropophagous barbarians.

CHAPTER EXAM ON AGREEMENT

Find all grammar errors and correct them most efficiently. The following sentences may contain one, multiple, or no error(s).

1)   Only when the young student who attends a very expensive private school receive~~s~~ a high score on the SAT ~~is~~ are his father, a prominent lawyer who works at one of the most prestigious law firms, and his mother, a respected doctor, likely to allow ~~her~~ their son to get a car.

2)   When the lady saw the majestic view, she ~~had felt~~felt a great renewing of her mind.

3)   By the time my sons and daughters reach the age of 40, all of them will have become ~~a missionary~~missionaries.

4)   By the time the girl and her grandmother finished that project which required a substantial amount of time, ~~she~~ the girl/her grandmother (ambiguous pronoun) ~~wrote~~ had written at least 9 creative papers.

5)   The special situations ~~where~~ in which my brazen cousin feels embarrassed ~~is~~ are hard to observe.

CHAPTER EXAM ON REDUNDANCY

Find all grammar errors and correct them most efficiently. The following sentences may contain one, multiple, or no error(s).

1)   When I couldn't understand the mechanism behind the ~~new~~ innovation, the developer repeated it ~~again~~ for me.

2)   This house has a ~~most~~ unique structure and is more ~~optimal~~ efficient than any other house.

3)   The new hybrid car will not, unless its price decreases, ~~hardly~~ sell to a sufficiently ~~enough~~ large number of consumers.

4)   "This is the ~~final~~ ultimatum!" shouted the general.

5)   The manager did not refer ~~back~~ to ~~nothing~~ anything special.

CHAPTER EXAM ON DICTION

Find all grammar errors and correct them most efficiently. The following sentences may contain one, multiple, or no error(s).

1) The accusations ~~lay~~ laid out in the media were preposterous and increasingly unbearable.

2) The ~~principle~~ principal reason ~~why~~ that North Korea still suffers under a dictator is ~~because~~ that its people are not sufficiently informed about how differently other people in the world live.

3) My sly cousin is ~~liable~~ likely to inherit a great amount of wealth from his grandfather, who is, despite having great business acumen, ~~credible~~credulous.

4) ~~Discreet~~ Discrete mathematics ~~compliments~~ complements continuous mathematics.

5) The riverside smelled quite ~~greatly~~ great from the ~~affect~~ effect of the revitalizing spring rain, and it was capable ~~to refresh~~of refreshing my mind.

COMPREHENSIVE EXAM ON OPTIMAL ENGLISH GRAMMAR

Find all grammar errors and correct them most efficiently. The following sentences may contain one, multiple, or no error(s).

1) Every one of the successful people ~~are~~ is characterized as well-organized and well-prepared for the matters ~~they want~~he/she wants ~~accomplishing~~ to accomplish; the lives of the majority of the prominent lawyers, CEOs, and doctors demonstrate that they are ~~a master~~masters of planning ahead for important events or projects.

2) While I cannot impugn the argument that too ~~many~~ much inflexible planning and execution may interfere with creativity that might arise at an unexpected moment, ~~if properly applied~~ I can unambiguously see that, if properly applied, great planning in fact can foster creativity.

3) Many of the great literary works, especially ~~novelists~~ novels and ~~biographers~~biographies, are creations from great planning and background research. ~~and~~ to make a creative and well-written story, an author must apply a period of intense cerebration and plotting ~~must be applied by an author~~ so that the story becomes novel and creative, full of both surprises and of interesting events.

4) Without great planning, authors are likely to ~~not only~~ produce not only an incoherent but also hackneyed and anticlimactic storyline that will leave the readers feeling exasperated~~ly~~ about ~~them~~ their wasting precious time.

5) Only by detailed planning ~~author~~ can an author minimize the unnecessary time cost of having to revise the entire book and the risk of publishing a ~~disappointed~~ disappointing book, thereby damaging ~~their~~ his or her reputation.

6) It is imperative that the director, ~~that~~ who is the planner, produce~~s~~ a memorable concert, and a~~n~~ unforgettable musical as well as ~~producing~~ a spectacular show, fraught with creative programs and events.

7) The blockbuster concerts or musicals that enjoy the ongoing utmost popularity ~~is~~ are ~~a product~~products of extensive and impeccable planning and coordinating ~~where~~ in which there is no room for error; not only the producers but also the director try hard~~ly~~ to meet the plan.

8) The planning team does ~~their~~ its best to incorporate creativity and innovations into the project; ~~but~~however, when the plan is finalized, all participants stick to the plan.

9) By meeting the expected course of action, ~~the audience can find that~~ the artists can maximally show the audience the intended creativity and quality; the viewers would ~~have shown~~show disappointment if they ~~would not have found~~did not find ~~it~~them.

10) There are, of course, some instances ~~when~~ in which spontaneous deviations from the plan must be allowed to produce the optimal result; for example, there are many jazz concerts ~~where~~ in which the musicians must be allowed to improvise according to the mood of the ambience and avoid~~ing~~ mechanically following ~~mechanically~~ premeditated actions.

11) Yet, even for this kind of occasion, ~~for maximizing~~to maximize the intended result, ~~great planning~~an artist must be capable ~~to take~~of taking into account all contingency plans~~;~~ ; therefore, I strongly believe that planning, ~~doing~~ done properly and thoroughly, do~~es~~ not ~~hardly~~ interfere with creativity.

12) Overall, planning can be beneficial: <u>Though</u> ~~An~~ <u>a</u> usual planner might not have the ability ~~of~~ <u>to</u> concoct~~ing~~ and ~~balancing~~ <u>balance</u> planning and creativity, a<u>n</u> honorable planner, ~~that~~ <u>who</u> is preoccupied ~~by~~ <u>with</u> making the perfect amalgamation, may use them as if they ~~are~~ <u>were</u> one and produce <u>a</u> ~~more~~ unique and optimal result ~~in~~ <u>with</u> which the audience fall<u>s</u> in love.

This book was dedicated to the One who is my everything.

77400197R00100

Made in the
USA
Columbia, SC